SAVVAS SUMMER IMPACT

Mathematics | Grade 2

SAVVAS
LEARNING COMPANY

MW01717447

Mathematicians

Roger Howe
Professor of Mathematics
Yale University
New Haven, Connecticut

Gary Lippman
Professor of Mathematics and Computer Science
California State University, East Bay
Hayward, California

ELL Consultants

Janice R. Corona
Independent Education Consultant
Dallas, Texas

Jim Cummins
Professor
The University of Toronto
Toronto, Canada

Reviewers

Katina Arnold
Teacher
Liberty Public School District
Kansas City, Missouri

Christy Bennett
Elementary Math and Science Specialist
DeSoto County Schools
Hernando, Mississippi

Shauna Bostick
Elementary Math Specialist
Lee County School District
Tupelo, Mississippi

Samantha Brant
Teacher
Platte County School District
Platte City, Missouri

Jamie Clark
Elementary Math Coach
Allegany County Public Schools
Cumberland, Maryland

Shauna Gardner
Math and Science Instructional Coach
DeSoto County Schools
Hernando, Mississippi

Kathy Graham
Educational Consultant
Twin Falls, Idaho

Andrea Hamilton
K-5 Math Specialist
Lake Forest School District
Felton, Delaware

Susan Hankins
Instructional Coach
Tupelo Public School District
Tupelo, Mississippi

Barb Jamison
Teacher
Excelsior Springs School District
Excelsior Springs, Missouri

Pam Jones
Elementary Math Coach
Lake Region School District
Bridgton, Maine

Sherri Kane
Secondary Mathematics Curriculum Specialist
Lee's Summit R7 School District
Lee's Summit, Missouri

Jessica Leonard
ESOL Teacher
Volusia County Schools
DeLand, Florida

Jill K. Milton
Elementary Math Coordinator
Norwood Public Schools
Norwood, Massachusetts

Jamie Pickett
Teacher
Platte County School District
Kansas City, Missouri

Mandy Schall
Math Coach
Allegany County Public Schools
Cumberland, Maryland

Marjorie Stevens
Math Consultant
Utica Community Schools
Shelby Township, Michigan

Shyree Stevenson
ELL Teacher
Penns Grove-Carneys Point Regional School District
Penns Grove, New Jersey

Kayla Stone
Teacher
Excelsior Springs School District
Excelsior Springs, Missouri

Sara Sultan
PD Academic Trainer, Math
Tucson Unified School District
Tucson, Arizona

Angela Waltrup
Elementary Math Content Specialist
Washington County Public Schools
Hagerstown, Maryland

Savvas Summer Impact Mathematics Grade 2 is a supplemental component of the enVision Math Program. Savvas Learning Company LLC, 15 East Midland Avenue, Paramus, NJ 07652

SAVVAS
LEARNING COMPANY

ISBN-13: 978-1-42848175-6
ISBN-10: 1-42-848175-3

1 21

Digital Resources

Go to SavvasRealize.com

Interactive Student Edition
Access online or offline.

Visual Learning
Interact with visual learning animations.

Activity
Solve a problem and share your thinking.

Interactive Additional Practice Workbook
Access online or offline.

Videos
Watch Another Look Videos.

Practice Buddy
Do interactice practice online.

Math Tools
Explore math with digital tools.

Games
Play math games to help you learn.

Glossary
Read and listen in English and Spanish.

Assessment
Show what you've learned.

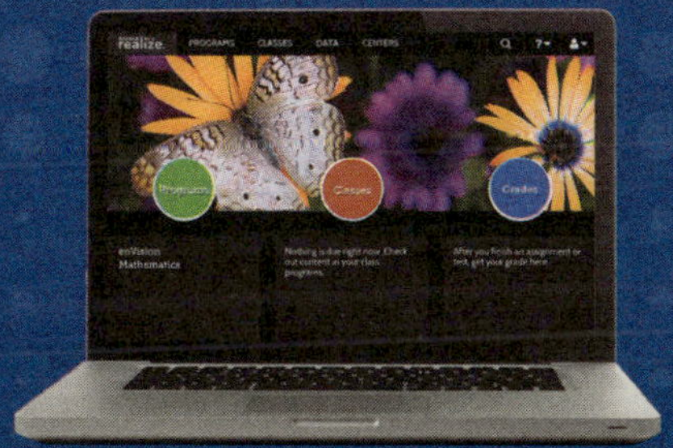

SAVVAS realize™ Everything you need for math anytime, anywhere

Hi, we're here to help you.
Let's have a great summer!
I'm Emily.
I'm Jada.
I'm Carlos.
I'm Marta.
I'm Jackson.
I'm Alex.
I'm Daniel.

Contents

LESSONS

1 (1-2) Doubles and Near Doubles 9
2 (1-3) Make a 10 to Add 13
3 (1-4) Addition Fact Patterns 17
4 (1-5) Count On and Count Back to Subtract 21
5 (1-6) Think Addition to Subtract 25
6 (1-7) Make a 10 to Subtract 29
7 (3-1) Add Tens and Ones on a Hundred Chart 93
8 (3-2) Add Tens and Ones on an Open Number Line 97
9 (3-3) Break Apart Numbers to Add 101
10 (3-4) Add Using Compensation 105
11 (4-1) Add 2-Digit Numbers Using Models 137
12 (4-2) Continue to Add 2-Digit Numbers Using Models 141
13 (4-3) Add with Partial Sums 145
14 (4-4) Add Using Mental Math and Partial Sums 149
15 (4-5) Break Apart Numbers and Add Using Mental Math 153

Contents

LESSONS

16 (5-1) Subtract Tens and Ones on a Hundred Chart 189

17 (5-2) Count Back to Subtract on an Open Number Line 193

18 (5-3) Add Up to Subtract Using an Open Number Line 197

19 (5-4) Break Apart Numbers to Subtract 201

20 (5-5) Subtract Using Compensation 205

21 (6-1) Subtract 1-Digit Numbers Using Models 237

22 (6-2) Subtract 2-Digit Numbers Using Models 241

23 (6-3) Subtract Using Partial Differences 245

24 (6-4) Continue to Subtract Using Partial Differences 249

25 (7-1) Represent Addition and Subtraction Problems 281

26 (7-2) Mixed Practice: Solve Addition and Subtraction Problems 285

27 (14-1) Add and Subtract with Measurements 609

28 (14-2) Find Unknown Measurements 613

29 (14-3) Continue to Find Unknown Measurements 617

30 (14-4) Add and Subtract on a Number Line 621

Name ____________________

Solve & Share

Use counters. Show 6 + 6 = 12.
Then show and explain how knowing that fact can help you find 6 + 7.

Lesson 1-2
Doubles and Near Doubles

I can ...
use doubles and near doubles to add quickly and accurately.

I can also look for patterns.

6 + 6 = 12 6 + 7 = ____

Visual Learning Bridge

Visual Learning | A-Z Glossary

Find 7 + 8 and find 7 + 9.

You can use the doubles fact to help find a **near doubles** fact.

Doubles Fact: 7 + 7 = 14

7 + 8 is 1 more than 7 + 7.

7 + 9 is 2 more than 7 + 7.

Convince Me! How could you use the doubles fact 7 + 7 to find 7 + 9?

Guided Practice Complete the doubles facts. Use the doubles facts to solve the near doubles. Use cubes if needed.

1. 2 + 2 = 4   2 + 3 = ____

2. ____ = 4 + 4   ____ = 4 + 5

3. $\begin{array}{r} 3 \\ +\ 3 \\ \hline \square \end{array}$ $\begin{array}{r} 3 \\ +\ 4 \\ \hline \square \end{array}$

4. $\begin{array}{r} 5 \\ +\ 5 \\ \hline \square \end{array}$ $\begin{array}{r} 5 \\ +\ 7 \\ \hline \square \end{array}$

Name ____________________

Tools Assessment

Independent Practice

Complete the doubles facts. Use the doubles facts to solve the near doubles. Use cubes if needed.

5. $6 + 6 =$ ____ $6 + 7 =$ ____

6. $5 + 5 =$ ____ $5 + 6 =$ ____

7. $8 + 8 =$ ____ $8 + 10 =$ ____

8. ____ $= 1 + 1$ ____ $= 1 + 3$

9. $\begin{array}{r} 2 \\ +\ 2 \\ \hline \square \end{array}$ $\begin{array}{r} 2 \\ +\ 3 \\ \hline \square \end{array}$

10. $\begin{array}{r} 4 \\ +\ 4 \\ \hline \square \end{array}$ $\begin{array}{r} 4 \\ +\ 5 \\ \hline \square \end{array}$

11. $\begin{array}{r} 8 \\ +\ 8 \\ \hline \square \end{array}$ $\begin{array}{r} 8 \\ +\ 9 \\ \hline \square \end{array}$

12. $\begin{array}{r} 3 \\ +\ 3 \\ \hline \square \end{array}$ $\begin{array}{r} 3 \\ +\ 5 \\ \hline \square \end{array}$

13. $\begin{array}{r} 5 \\ +\ 5 \\ \hline \square \end{array}$ $\begin{array}{r} 5 \\ +\ 7 \\ \hline \square \end{array}$

14. $\begin{array}{r} 7 \\ +\ 7 \\ \hline \square \end{array}$ $\begin{array}{r} 7 \\ +\ 9 \\ \hline \square \end{array}$

15. Algebra Complete. Then explain how you solved the problem.

$9 + \square = 18$ $\square + \square = 19$

____

____

____

Problem Solving Solve the problems below.

16. Model John drew 4 houses. Then he drew 5 more houses. How many houses did John draw in all?

Draw a picture and write an equation to explain your thinking.

____ ◯ ____ = ____ houses

17. Higher Order Thinking Choose a doubles fact. Use that doubles fact to draw a picture that shows a near doubles story. Write the near doubles fact.

18. Assessment Practice Kate wants to find 6 + 7.

Which doubles fact will help her the most?

Ⓐ 4 + 4 = 8

Ⓑ 6 + 6 = 12

Ⓒ 8 + 8 = 16

Ⓓ 9 + 9 = 18

Name ______________________

Activity

Lesson 1-3

Make a 10 to Add

I can ...
make a 10 to help me add quickly and accurately.

I can also reason about math.

Solve & Share

How can thinking about 10 help you find 9 + 3?
Use the ten-frames and counters to show how.

$$\begin{array}{r} 9 \\ +\ 3 \\ \hline \square \end{array}$$

Visual Learning   A-Z Glossary

You can make a 10 to help you add.

$$\begin{array}{r} 8 \\ +\ 5 \\ \hline ? \end{array}$$

Move 2 counters to make a 10.

Add with 10.

Convince Me! Why do you move 2 counters to add 8 + 5?

Guided Practice

Make a 10 to add.
Use counters and ten-frames.

1. $$\begin{array}{r} 7 \\ +\ 4 \\ \hline ? \end{array}$$

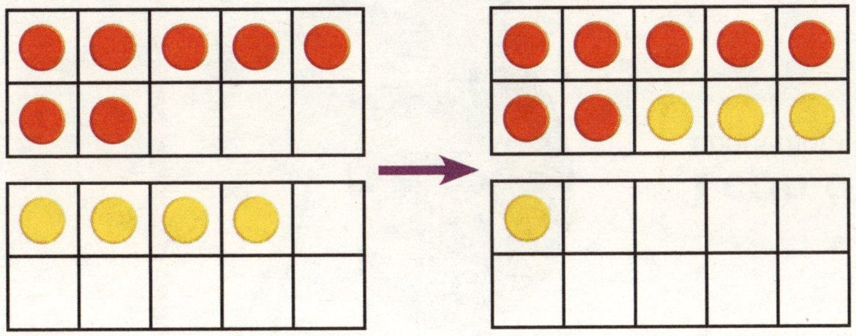

$$\begin{array}{r} 10 \\ +\ 1 \\ \hline 11 \end{array} \quad \text{so,} \quad \begin{array}{r} 7 \\ +\ \square \\ \hline \square \end{array}$$

Name ______________________________

Independent Practice

Make a 10 to add. Use counters and ten-frames.

2. 8 + 4 = ☐

3. 3 + 9 = ☐

4. 6 + 7 = ☐

5. 5 + 8 = ☐

6. 7 + 5 = ☐

7. 5 + 9 = ____

8. 3 + 8 = ____

9. 4 + 9 = ____

10. 7 + 9 = ____

Algebra Which number is missing?

11. 8 + 5 = ☐ + 3

12. 6 + 9 = 10 + ☐

13. 8 + 9 = 10 + ☐

14. **Higher Order Thinking** Can you make a 10 to help you add 7 + 4 + 5? Explain.

____

____

____

Problem Solving

Solve the problems below. Show your work.

15. Tan's team scored 16 points in a game. During the first half, they scored 9 points. How many points did the team score in the second half of the game?

_____ points

16. **Make Sense** The school has a clothing drive for charity. Ana's class donates 8 coats. Nico's class donates 5 hats. Adam's class donates 8 coats. How many coats were donated in all?

_____ coats

17. **Higher Order Thinking** Draw a picture to show how you can make a 10 to help you add 3 + 5 + 9. Explain your picture to a friend.

18. **Assessment Practice** Use the ten-frames. Show how to find 5 + 7 by making a 10. Then fill in the gray boxes.

$$\begin{array}{r} 5 \\ +\ 7 \\ \hline \square \end{array}$$

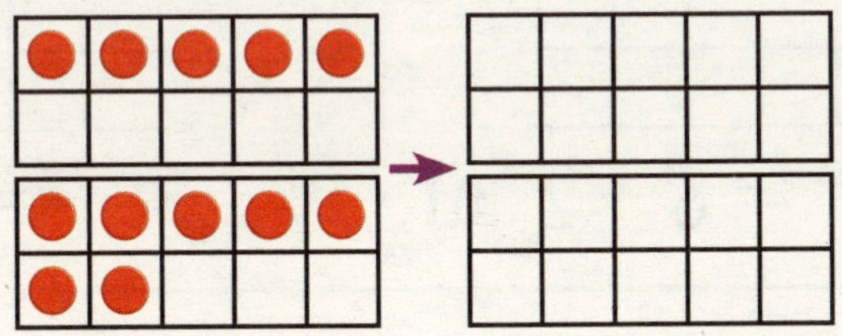

$$\begin{array}{r} 10 \\ +\ \square \\ \hline \square \end{array}$$

Name ____________________

Solve & Share

Look at the sums on an addition facts table for addends 0 to 5. Describe one of the patterns that you see. Use words, colors, or addition facts to describe the patterns.

Activity

Lesson 1-4

Addition Fact Patterns

I can ...
use the patterns on an addition facts table to help me remember the addition facts.

I can also look for patterns.

+	0	1	2	3	4	5
0	0	1	2	3	4	5
1	1	2	3	4	5	6
2	2	3	4	5	6	7
3	3	4	5	6	7	8
4	4	5	6	7	8	9
5	5	6	7	8	9	10

____

____

____

____

Visual Learning | A-Z Glossary

Visual Learning Bridge

How can you describe a pattern for all the sums of six?

+	0	1	2	3	4	5	6	7	8	9	10
0	0	1	2	3	4	5	6	7	8	9	10
1	1	2	3	4	5	6	7	8	9	10	11
2	2	3	4	5	6	7	8	9	10	11	12
3	3	4	5	6	7	8	9	10	11	12	13
4	4	5	6	7	8	9	10	11	12	13	14
5	5	6	7	8	9	10	11	12	13	14	15
6	6	7	8	9	10	11	12	13	14	15	16
7	7	8	9	10	11	12	13	14	15	16	17
8	8	9	10	11	12	13	14	15	16	17	18
9	9	10	11	12	13	14	15	16	17	18	19
10	10	11	12	13	14	15	16	17	18	19	20

You can write an addition equation.
4 + 2 = 6
4 and 2 are addends for the sum of 6.

+	0	1	2	3	4
0	0	1	2	3	4
1	1	2	3	4	5
2	2	3	4	5	6

Here are all the ways to make a sum of 6.
6 + 0 = 6
5 + 1 = 6
4 + 2 = 6
3 + 3 = 6
2 + 4 = 6
1 + 5 = 6
0 + 6 = 6

Convince Me! How can patterns on an addition facts table help you remember the addition facts? Explain.

Guided Practice

Use fact patterns to complete each equation.

1. 10 + 6 = 16
9 + 7 = 16
8 + 8 = 16
7 + 9 = 16
6 + 10 = 16

2. 10 + ___ = 14
___ + 5 = 14
8 + 6 = ___
7 + ___ = 14
___ + 8 = 14
5 + ___ = 14
___ + 10 = 14

3. 9 + ___ = 9
___ + 1 = 9
7 + 2 = ___
6 + ___ = 9
___ + 4 = 9
5 + ___ = 9
___ + 3 = 9
___ + 2 = 9
8 + 1 = ___
___ + 0 = 9

Name ______________________________

Tools Assessment

Independent Practice

Use fact patterns to complete each equation.

4. 10 + ___ = 12
___ + 3 = 12
8 + 4 = ___
7 + ___ = 12
6 + 6 = ___
___ + 7 = 12
4 + ___ = 12
___ + 9 = 12

5. 7 + ___ = 7
___ + 1 = 7
5 + 2 = ___
___ + 3 = 7
___ + 4 = 7
___ + 5 = 7
___ + 6 = 7
0 + ___ = 7

6. 10 + ___ = 15
___ + 5 = 15
9 + 6 = ___
9 + ___ = 15
7 + ___ = 15
___ + 8 = 15

7. **Number Sense** Find the 8 in the top row of the addition facts table. Complete all of the equations using the 8-column on the table. What pattern do you see?

8 + ___ = 8
8 + ___ = 9
8 + ___ = 10
8 + 3 = ___
8 + ___ = 12
8 + ___ = ___

8 + 6 = ___
8 + ___ = 15
8 + 8 = ___
8 + ___ = ___
8 + 10 = ___

____
____
____
____

Problem Solving

Solve the problems below.

8. **Reasoning** Lucy is sorting items by their texture. She finds 6 items that are bumpy. Lucy finds 5 items that are smooth. How many items does Lucy find in all?

_____ items

9. **Vocabulary** Look at the **equation** below. Circle the **addends**. Draw a square around the **sum**.

9 + 5 = 14

10. **Higher Order Thinking** Write 8 addition facts that have a sum of 12. How can the addition patterns help you? Explain.

11. **Assessment Practice** Which have a sum of 17? Choose all that apply.

- ☐ 10 + 7 = ?
- ☐ 7 + 6 = ?
- ☐ 9 + 8 = ?
- ☐ 8 + 8 = ?

Name ______________________________

Lesson 1-5

Count On and Count Back to Subtract

I can ...
count on and count back on a number line to subtract.

I can also reason about math.

Solve & Share

How can counting help you find 12 – 4? Use the number line to show your work.

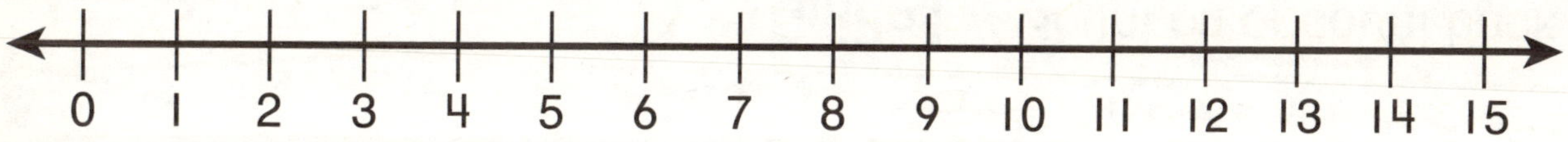

12 – 4 = ______

Visual Learning | A-Z Glossary

Visual Learning Bridge

Find 10 – 4. Start with the lesser number.

Count on to 10 to find the **difference**.

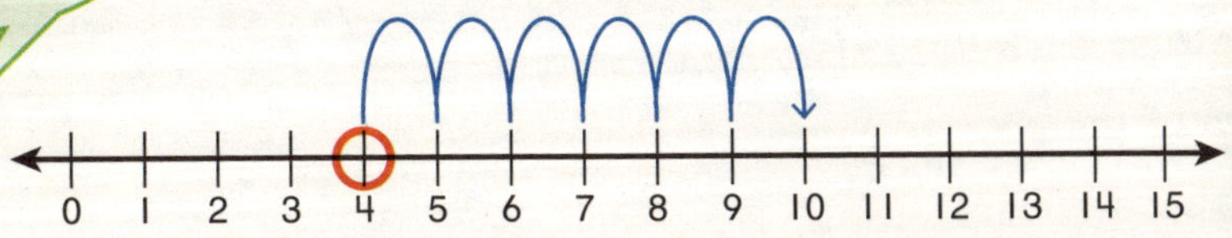

4, 5, 6, 7, 8, 9, 10

It takes 6 moves to count on from 4 to 10.

So, 10 – 4 = 6.

You can also count back to subtract.

Start with the greater number.

Count back 4 moves.

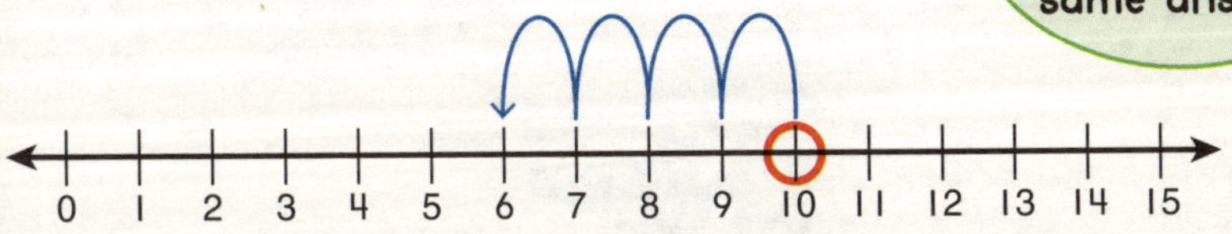

10, 9, 8, 7, 6

You land on 6. So, 10 – 4 = 6.

Convince Me! How can you count back on a number line to find 9 – 5?

Guided Practice Count on or count back to subtract. Show your work on the number line.

1. 11 – 4 = 7

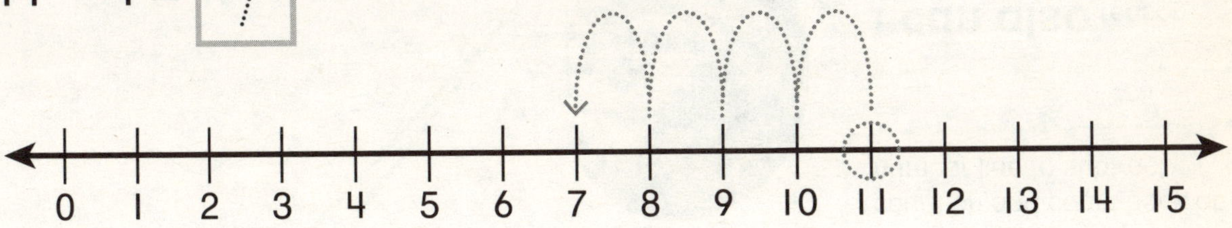

2. 14 – 7 = ☐

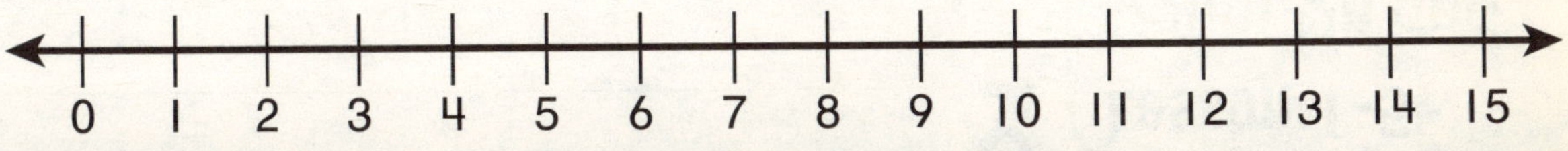

Name ______________________________

Tools Assessment

Independent Practice

Count on or count back to subtract. Show your work on the number line.

3. 14 – 8 = ☐

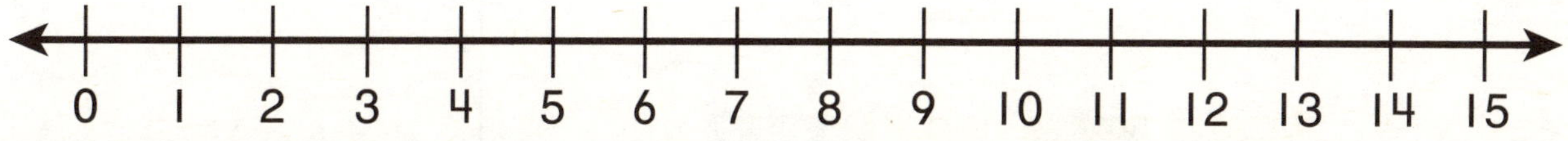

4. 12 – 7 = ☐

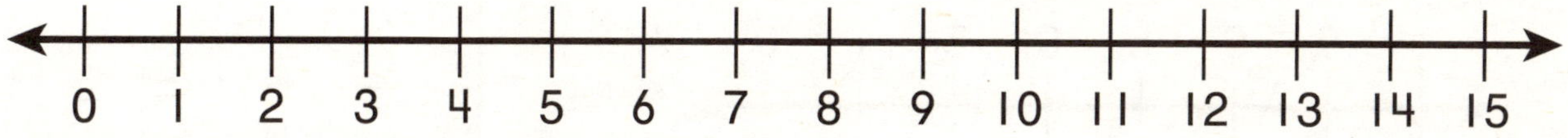

5. 9 – 7 = ☐

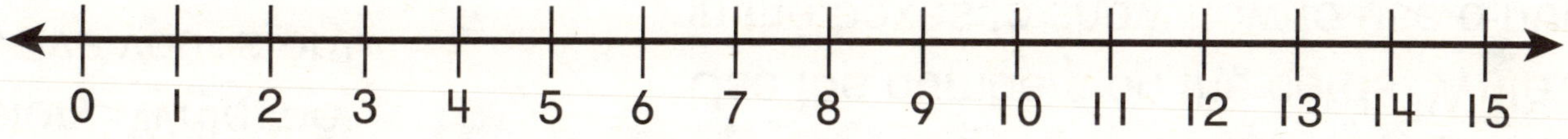

6. 15 – 6 = ☐

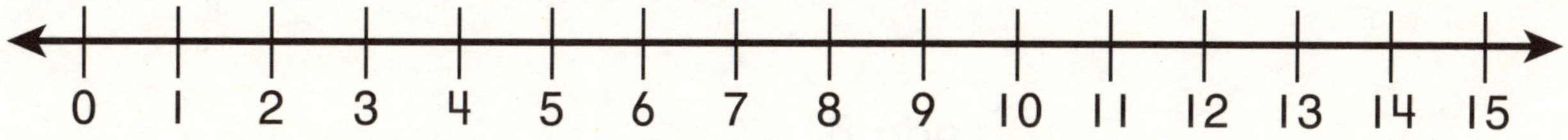

7. **Higher Order Thinking** How can you count on to find 13 – 4? Explain.

____

____

____

Problem Solving

Solve the problems below.

8. Callie had 18 seeds. She planted 10 of the seeds. How many seeds does Callie have now?

_____ seeds

9. Make Sense Peter has 16 grapes. He eats some of the grapes. Peter has 10 grapes left. How many grapes did Peter eat?

_____ grapes

10. Higher Order Thinking Choose 2 numbers. Use the numbers to write or draw a subtraction story. Write the equation you used to solve your story.

_____ − _____ = _____

11. Assessment Practice Jake wants to find 6 − 3.

Use the numbers on the cards. Write them in the boxes to show how to use a number line to count on to solve.

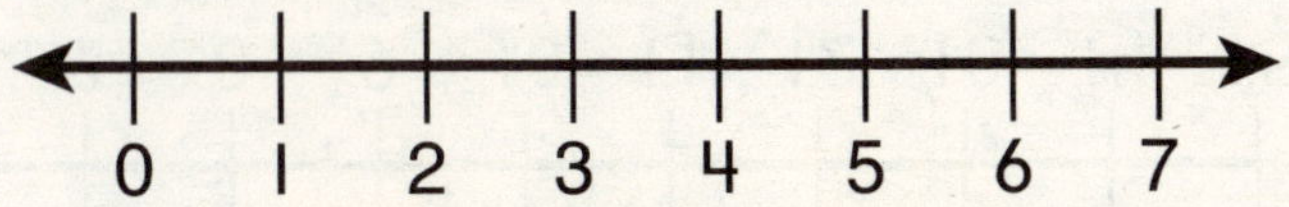

6 3 5 4

Begin with ☐. Then count on, ☐, ☐, ☐.

6 − 3 = _____

Name ______________________________

Lesson 1-6

Think Addition to Subtract

I can ...
use addition to help me subtract quickly and accurately.

I can also reason about math.

Solve & Share

How can you use an addition fact to find 14 – 6? Use counters to help show how.

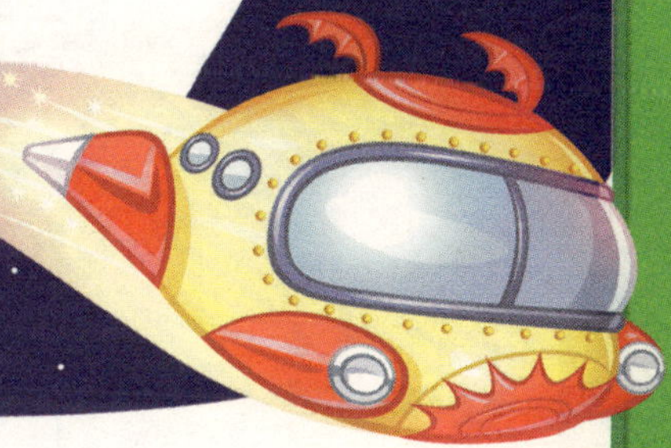

____ + ____ = ____

So, 14 – 6 = ____.

Visual Learning | A-Z Glossary

Visual Learning Bridge

Find 15 – 7.

To find 15 – 7, you can think:

The missing number is the same in both equations.

7 + ___ = 15

15 – 7 = ___

You know the addition fact.

7 + 8 = 15

You also know the subtraction fact.

15 – 7 = 8

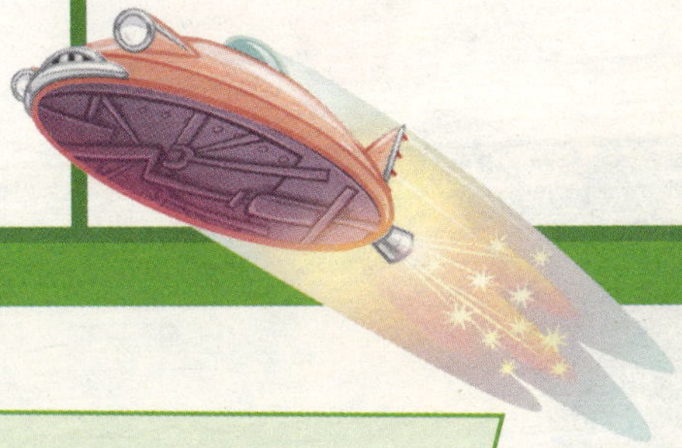

Convince Me! How do you know which addition fact to use to complete the subtraction fact?

Guided Practice

Think addition to help you subtract.

1. 6 – 4 = ?

   4 + 2 = 6

   So, 6 – 4 = 2.

2. 9 – 3 = ?

   3 + ___ = 9

   So, 9 – 3 = ___.

3. 14 – 5 = ?

   5 + ___ = 14

   So, 14 – 5 = ___.

4. 12 – 4 = ?

   4 + ___ = 12

   So, 12 – 4 = ___.

Name ______________________________

Tools Assessment

Independent Practice

Subtract. Complete the addition fact that can help you.

5. $8 - 1 =$ ____

$1 +$ ____ $= 8$

6. $10 - 2 =$ ____

$2 +$ ____ $= 10$

7. $15 - 6 =$ ____

$6 +$ ____ $= 15$

8. $17 - 7 =$ ____

$7 +$ ____ $= 17$

9. $14 - 8 =$ ____

$8 +$ ____ $= 14$

10. $9 - 5 =$ ____

$5 +$ ____ $= 9$

11. $\begin{array}{r} 18 \\ -\ 8 \\ \hline \square \end{array}$ $\quad$ $\begin{array}{r} 8 \\ +\ \square \\ \hline 18 \end{array}$

12. $\begin{array}{r} 16 \\ -\ 9 \\ \hline \square \end{array}$ $\quad$ $\begin{array}{r} 9 \\ +\ \square \\ \hline 16 \end{array}$

13. $\begin{array}{r} 19 \\ -\ 9 \\ \hline \square \end{array}$ $\quad$ $\begin{array}{r} 9 \\ +\ \square \\ \hline 19 \end{array}$

Higher Order Thinking

Write a related addition fact to complete the subtraction fact.

14. $11 -$ ____ $= 5$

____ $+$ ____ $=$ ____

15. $7 -$ ____ $= 2$

____ $+$ ____ $=$ ____

16. $12 -$ ____ $= 8$

____ $+$ ____ $=$ ____

Problem Solving

Solve the problems below. Write an equation.

17. Reasoning Kate had 6 pens. She got 5 more pens from John. How many pens does Kate have in all?

____ ◯ ____ = ____

____ pens

18. Reasoning John had 11 pens. He gave 5 pens to Kate. How many pens does John have now?

____ ◯ ____ = ____

____ pens

19. Higher Order Thinking Write a subtraction story using the numbers 18 and 10. Then write an addition fact that can help you solve the problem in your story.

____ + ____ = ____

20. Assessment Practice Pam has 16 cherries. She eats 7 cherries. Which addition fact can help you find how many cherries Pam has left?

Ⓐ 7 + 4 = 11

Ⓑ 7 + 6 = 13

Ⓒ 7 + 9 = 16

Ⓓ 9 + 9 = 18

Name ____________________

Activity

Lesson 1-7

Make a 10 to Subtract

I can ...
make a 10 to help me subtract quickly and accurately.

I can also make math arguments.

Solve & Share

14 ladybugs are on a leaf. 6 ladybugs fly away. How can thinking about 10 help you find how many ladybugs are left? Explain.

_____ ◯ _____ = _____

Visual Learning | A-Z Glossary

Visual Learning Bridge

Find 13 − 7. You can use 10 to help you subtract.

One way is to start with 7 and add 3 to get to 10.

7 + 3 = 10

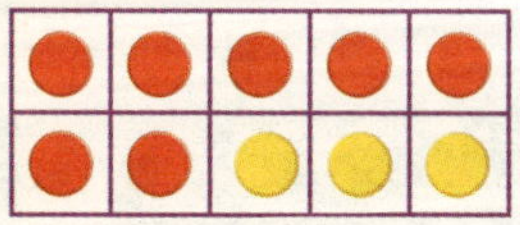

Next, add 3 more to make 13.

10 + 3 = 13

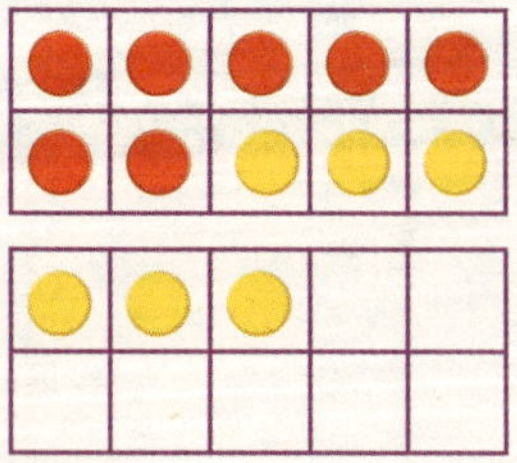

7 + 6 = 13,
so 13 − 7 = 6.

Another way is to start with 13 and subtract 3 to get to 10.

13 − 3 = 10

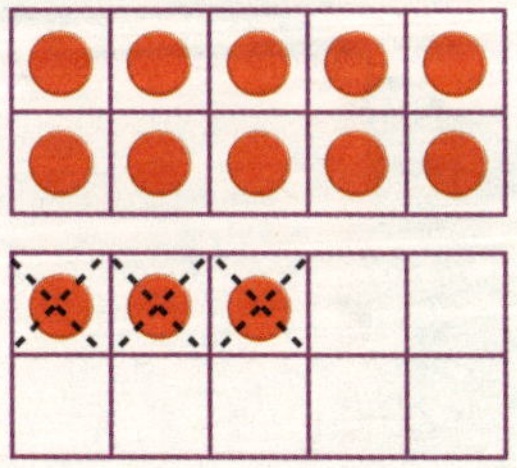

Since 3 + 4 = 7, subtract 4 more.

10 − 4 = 6

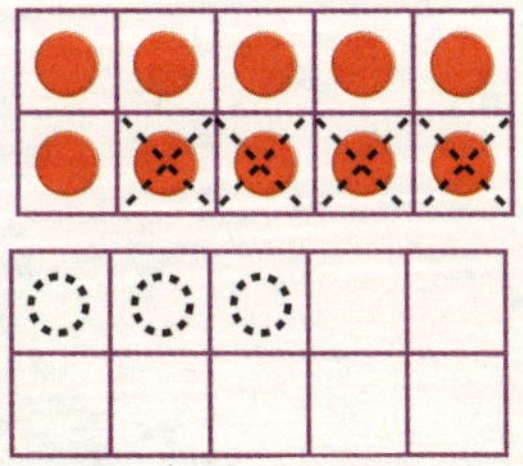

So, 13 − 7 = 6.

Convince Me! Do you prefer to add first to get to 10 or subtract first to get to 10? Explain.

Guided Practice

Make a 10 to subtract.
Use counters and your workmat.

1. First add to get to 10.

$$\begin{array}{r} 15 \\ -\ 8 \\ \hline 7 \end{array}$$

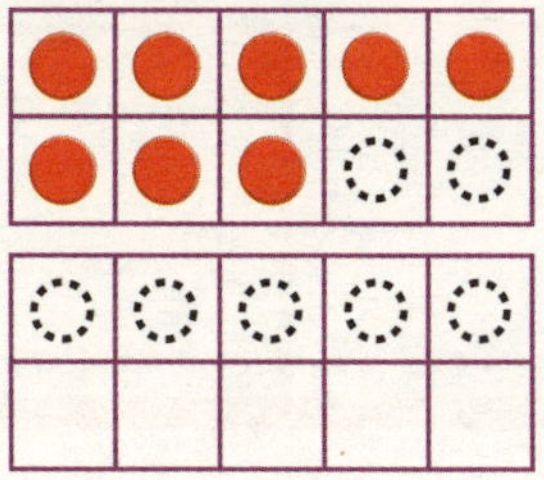

$$\begin{array}{r} 8 \\ +\ \boxed{2} \\ \hline 10 \end{array} \qquad \begin{array}{r} 10 \\ +\ \boxed{5} \\ \hline 15 \end{array}$$

2. First subtract to get to 10.

$$\begin{array}{r} 16 \\ -\ 7 \\ \hline \end{array}$$

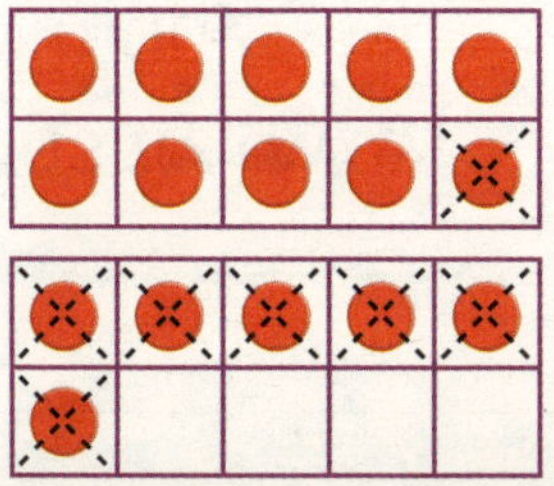

$$\begin{array}{r} 16 \\ -\ \boxed{} \\ \hline 10 \end{array} \qquad \begin{array}{r} 10 \\ -\ \boxed{} \\ \hline 9 \end{array}$$

Name ______________________

Tools Assessment

Independent Practice

Make a 10 to subtract. Use counters and your workmat.

3. $\begin{array}{r} 11 \\ -\ 4 \\ \hline \end{array}$

4. $\begin{array}{r} 14 \\ -\ 8 \\ \hline \end{array}$

5. $\begin{array}{r} 12 \\ -\ 7 \\ \hline \end{array}$

6. $\begin{array}{r} 12 \\ -\ 4 \\ \hline \end{array}$

7. $\begin{array}{r} 18 \\ -\ 9 \\ \hline \end{array}$

8. $\begin{array}{r} 17 \\ -\ 8 \\ \hline \end{array}$

9. $\begin{array}{r} 16 \\ -\ 8 \\ \hline \end{array}$

10. $\begin{array}{r} 13 \\ -\ 4 \\ \hline \end{array}$

11. $\begin{array}{r} 15 \\ -\ 9 \\ \hline \end{array}$

12. $\begin{array}{r} 14 \\ -\ 7 \\ \hline \end{array}$

13. $\begin{array}{r} 12 \\ -\ 8 \\ \hline \end{array}$

14. $\begin{array}{r} 16 \\ -\ 9 \\ \hline \end{array}$

15. **Higher Order Thinking** Carol subtracts 6 from 15. First, she adds to get to 10. Then she adds again to find her answer. Her answer is 10. Is Carol correct? Explain.

____

____

____

____

Problem Solving

Solve each problem. Which tool would you use?

16. **Use Tools** Chen had 12 animal stickers. He gave 5 of the stickers away. How many animal stickers does Chen have now?

_____ animal stickers

17. **Use Tools** Angie bought 13 strawberries. She ate 8 of the strawberries. How many strawberries does Angie have now?

_____ strawberries

18. **Higher Order Thinking** Show how you can make a 10 to find 17 – 9. Then explain your work.

19. **Assessment Practice** Use the ten-frames. Show how to make a 10 to find 15 – 9. Start by subtracting to get to 10. Then complete the equations.

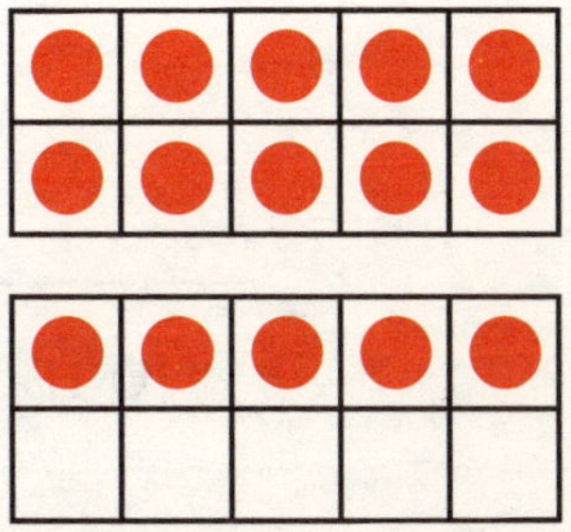

15 – _____ = 10

10 – _____ = _____ So, 15 – 9 = _____.

Name ______________________________

Activity

Lesson 3-1

Add Tens and Ones on a Hundred Chart

I can ...
add within 100 using place-value strategies and properties of operations.

I can also make math arguments.

Solve & Share

How can you use the hundred chart to help you find 32 + 43? Explain.

Write an equation to show the sum.

1	2	3	4	5	6	7	8	9	10
11	12	13	14	15	16	17	18	19	20
21	22	23	24	25	26	27	28	29	30
31	32	33	34	35	36	37	38	39	40
41	42	43	44	45	46	47	48	49	50
51	52	53	54	55	56	57	58	59	60
61	62	63	64	65	66	67	68	69	70
71	72	73	74	75	76	77	78	79	80
81	82	83	84	85	86	87	88	89	90
91	92	93	94	95	96	97	98	99	100

_____ + _____ = _____

Visual Learning A-Z Glossary

Visual Learning Bridge

You can add on a hundred chart. Find 54 + 18.

One Way Add the tens first.

Start at 54. Add 18.
Move down 1 row to add 1 ten.
Then move ahead 8 to add 8 ones.
54 + 18 = 72

51	52	53	54	55	56	57	58	59	60
61	62	63	64	65	66	67	68	69	70
71	72	73	74	75	76	77	78	79	80

Another Way Add the ones first.

Start at 54. Add 18.
Move ahead 8 to add 8 ones.
Then move down 1 row to add 1 ten.
54 + 18 = 72
I get the same sum both ways!

51	52	53	54	55	56	57	58	59	60
61	62	63	64	65	66	67	68	69	70
71	72	73	74	75	76	77	78	79	80

Convince Me! Max says that to find 54 + 18 on a hundred chart, you can start at 54, move down 2 rows, and move back 2 spaces. Do you agree? Explain.

Guided Practice Add using the hundred chart. Draw arrows on the chart if needed.

11	12	13	14	15	16	17	18	19	20
21	22	23	24	25	26	27	28	29	30
31	32	33	34	35	36	37	38	39	40
41	42	43	44	45	46	47	48	49	50

1. 17 + 32 = 49

2. 28 + 21 = ____

3. ____ = 19 + 20

4. 18 + 8 = ____

Name ______

Tools Assessment

Independent Practice

Add using the hundred chart.

1	2	3	4	5	6	7	8	9	10
11	12	13	14	15	16	17	18	19	20
21	22	23	24	25	26	27	28	29	30
31	32	33	34	35	36	37	38	39	40
41	42	43	44	45	46	47	48	49	50
51	52	53	54	55	56	57	58	59	60
61	62	63	64	65	66	67	68	69	70
71	72	73	74	75	76	77	78	79	80
81	82	83	84	85	86	87	88	89	90
91	92	93	94	95	96	97	98	99	100

5. 33 + 9 = ______

6. ______ = 12 + 73

7. 38 + 21 = ______

8. 56 + 42 = ______

9. ______ = 47 + 28

10. 39 + 17 = ______

11. ______ = 61 + 19

12. Higher Order Thinking Write the digit that makes each equation true.

☐ + 83 = 90   34 + 2☐ = 57   1☐ + 51 = 67   62 + ☐1 = 83

Problem Solving

Use Tools Use the hundred chart to solve the problems.

13. Sara has 48 buttons. Luis has 32 buttons. How many buttons do they have in all?

_____ buttons

31	32	33	34	35	36	37	38	39	40
41	42	43	44	45	46	47	48	49	50
51	52	53	54	55	56	57	58	59	60
61	62	63	64	65	66	67	68	69	70
71	72	73	74	75	76	77	78	79	80
81	82	83	84	85	86	87	88	89	90
91	92	93	94	95	96	97	98	99	100

14. Mika had 70 buttons. Then she found 19 more buttons. How many buttons does Mika have now?

_____ buttons

15. **Higher Order Thinking** Write the steps you take to add 43 and 39 on a hundred chart.

16. **Assessment Practice** Which has a sum of 35? Choose all that apply.

- ☐ 15 + 20
- ☐ 16 + 19
- ☐ 20 + 15
- ☐ 30 + 15

Name ______________________________

Solve & Share

How can you use the open number line to find 35 + 24?

Write an equation to show the sum. Explain your work.

____ + ____ = ____

Activity

Lesson 3-2

Add Tens and Ones on an Open Number Line

I can ...

use an open number line to add tens and ones within 100.

I can also reason about math.

Visual Learning | A-Z Glossary

Visual Learning Bridge

Find 48 + 23. Use an **open number line**.

One Way

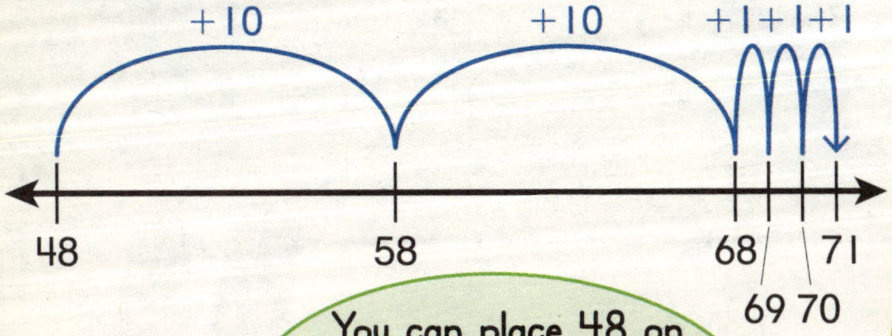

You can place 48 on the number line. Then count on 2 tens and 3 ones to add 23.

Another Way

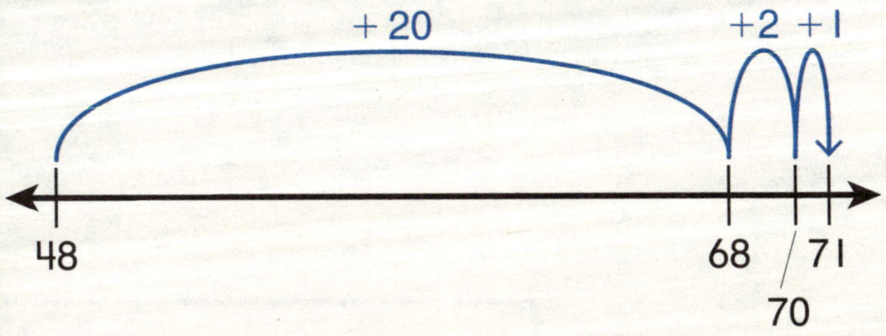

So, 48 + 23 = 71.

There are many ways to do it. This way shows a jump of 20, then 2, then 1 to add 23. Both ways land on 71.

Convince Me! Explain how you can use an open number line to find 56 + 35.

Guided Practice Use an open number line to find each sum.

1. 59 + 24 = ____

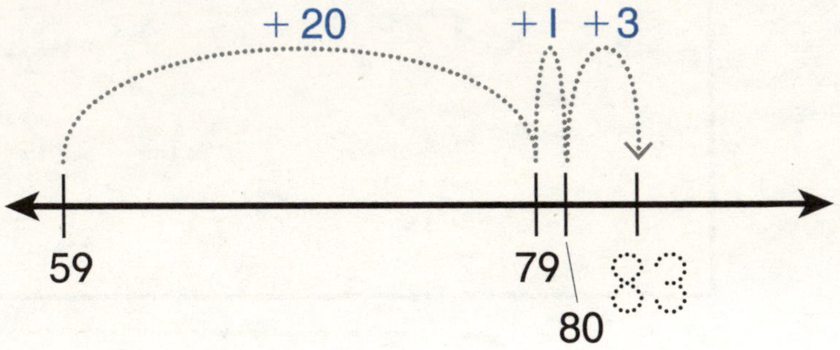

2. 47 + 25 = ____

Name ______________________________

Independent Practice

Use an open number line to find each sum.

3. 34 + 15 = ______

4. 34 + 46 = ______

5. 16 + 28 = ______

6. 59 + 26 = ______

7. **Number Sense** Matt found 55 + 28 using the open number line below. Is his work correct? Explain.

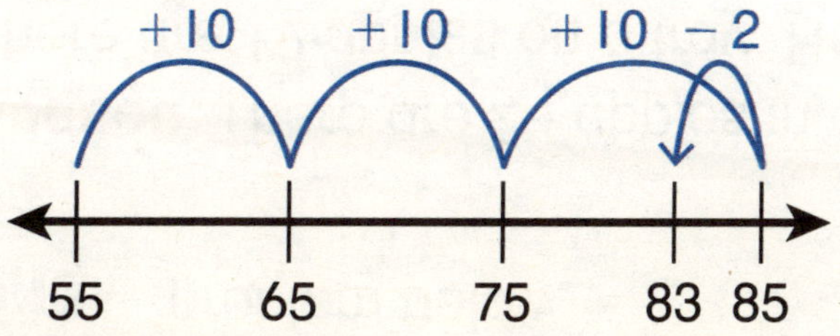

Problem Solving Use the open number line to solve each problem below.

8. **Reason** There are 24 apples in a basket. There are 19 apples on a tray. How many apples are there in all?

_____ apples

9. **Reason** Jamie has 27 more berries than Lisa. Lisa has 37 berries. How many berries does Jamie have?

_____ berries

10. **Higher Order Thinking** Use two different number lines to show that 34 + 23 has the same value as 23 + 34.

11. **Assessment Practice** Use the numbers on the cards. Write the missing numbers under the number line to show how to find the sum.

63 68 43 53

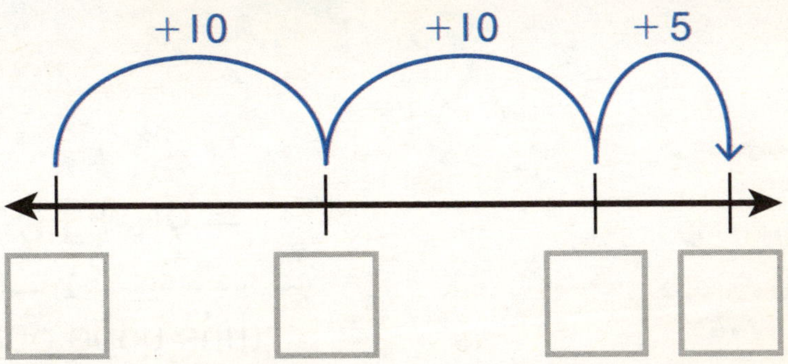

43 + 25 = _____

Name ______________________

Solve & Share

Josh has 34 cans to recycle. Jill has 27 cans. How many cans do they have in all?

Solve any way you choose. Use drawings and equations to explain your work.

Lesson 3-3

Break Apart Numbers to Add

I can ...

break apart numbers into tens and ones to find their sum.

I can also model with math.

____ ◯ ____ = ____ cans

Visual Learning A-Z Glossary

Visual Learning Bridge

37 + 25 = ?

You can **break apart** just the second addend into **tens** and **ones**.

37 + 25 = ?

37 | 20 | 5

Start at one addend. Add the **tens** and **ones** of the second addend.

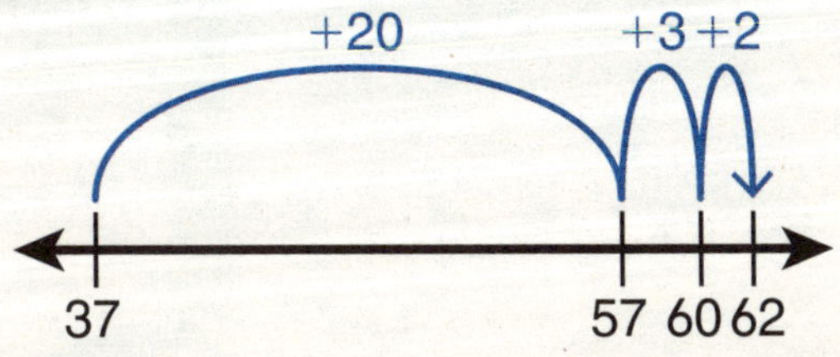

37 + **20** = 57

57 + **3** = 60

60 + **2** = 62

So, 37 + 25 = 62.

Convince Me! Explain how you can break apart 28 to find 33 + 28.

Guided Practice Break apart the second addend to find the sum. Show your work. Use an open number line to help.

1. 57 + 13 = ____

57 | 10 | 3

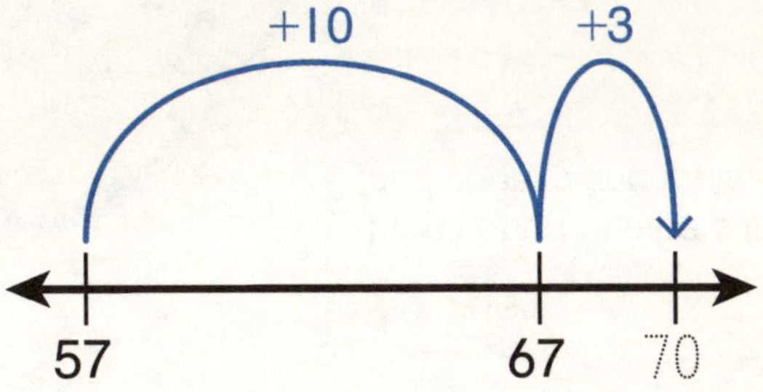

57 + 10 = 67

67 + 3 = 70

Name ______________________________

Tools Assessment

Independent Practice

Break apart the second addend to find the sum. Show your work. Draw an open number line to help.

2. 42 + 16 = ____

3. 36 + 44 = ____

4. 41 + 37 = ____

5. 35 + 47 = ____

6. 32 + 28 = ____

7. 48 + 27 = ____

8. **Number Sense** Write the digit that makes each equation true.

36 + 5☐ = 88

28 + 4☐ = 75

14 + 4☐ = 57

53 + 2☐ = 82

Problem Solving

Solve each problem. Show your work.

9. Amir planted 35 trees.
Juan planted 27 trees.
How many trees did they plant in all?

_____ trees

10. Carmen has 18 pennies.
Patrick has 12 more pennies than Carmen.
How many pennies does Patrick have?

_____ pennies

11. **Higher Order Thinking** Use the numbers on the cards. Use each number once to write a true equation.

3 2 8

5 ☐ + ☐ 4 = ☐ 6

12. **Assessment Practice** Which has a sum of 67? Choose all that apply.

- ☐ 15 + 52
- ☐ 15 + 62
- ☐ 38 + 29
- ☐ 11 + 55

Name ______

Solve & Share

$27 + 16 =$ ____

Draw counters on the ten-frames to show each addend.

Then show how you can move some counters to make it easier to find the sum.

Explain your work.

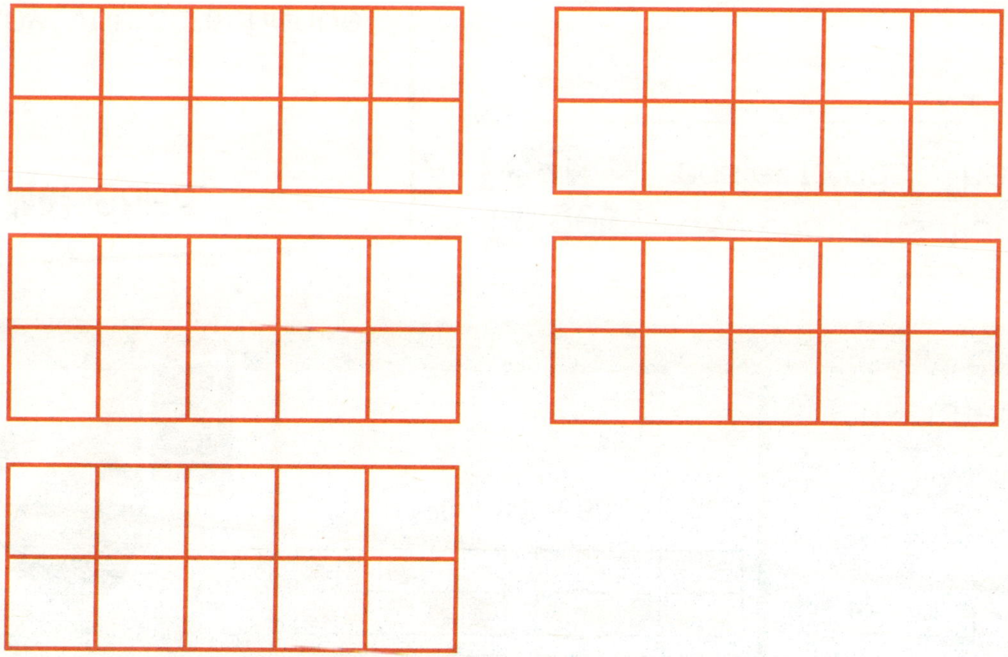

$27 + 16 =$ ____

Activity

Lesson 3-4

Add Using Compensation

I can ...
break apart addends and combine them in different ways to make numbers that are easy to add mentally.

I can also reason about math.

Visual Learning A-Z Glossary

Visual Learning Bridge

Find 18 + 15.

One way Take 2 from 15 and give it to 18 to make 20.

18 + 15 = ?

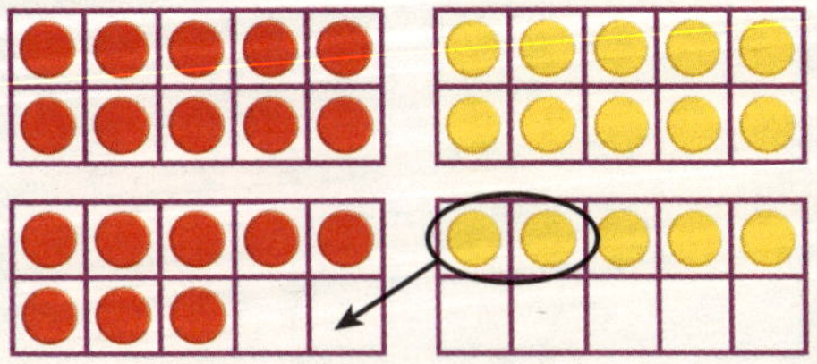

20 + 13 = 33

Show how you changed the numbers to make them easier to add.

18 + 15 = ?
+2 −2
20 + 13
10 + 3
20 + 10 + 3 = 33

So, 20 + 13 = 33.

18 + 15 = 20 + 13

So, 18 + 15 = 33.

Convince Me! Solve.

19 + 26 = ☐

Explain how you can change the addends to make them easier to add.

Guided Practice Use compensation to make numbers that are easier to add. Then solve. Show your work.

1. 17 + 9 = ____
(+) 3 (−) 3
20 + 6 = 26

2. 16 + 14 = ____
( ) ____ ( ) ____
____ + ____ = ____

Name ______

Tools Assessment

Independent Practice

Use compensation to make numbers that are easier to add. Then solve. Show your work.

3. 33 + 19 = ______

4. 28 + 8 = ______

5. 27 + 36 = ______

6. **Number Sense** Explain how you can use compensation to make numbers that are easy to add. Solve. Show your work.

28 + 37 = ☐

______ + ______ = ☐

7. **Higher Order Thinking** Show two different ways you could use compensation to make numbers that are easy to add. Solve. Show your work.

17 + 26 = ☐

Problem Solving

Use compensation to make numbers that are easier to add. Then solve. Show your work.

8. **Explain** Bella said there is only one way to rewrite this problem to make the numbers easier to add. Is she correct? Explain. Then solve.

$42 + 29 = \square$

9. **Vocabulary** Show two different ways to use **compensation** to find the sum. Then solve.

$58 + 35 = \square$

10. **Higher Order Thinking** Show two different ways to use compensation to find the sum. Then solve.

$37 + 16 + 5 = \square$

11. **Assessment Practice** Which is equal to 42 + 18? Choose all that apply.

- ☐ 58
- ☐ 40 + 20
- ☐ 40 + 10 + 8
- ☐ 50 + 10

Name ______________________

Solve & Share

Activity

Lesson 4-1
Add 2-Digit Numbers Using Models

I can ...
use models to add 2-digit numbers and then explain my work.

I can also use math tools correctly.

Leslie collects 36 rocks. Her brother collects 27 rocks. How many rocks do they collect in all?

Use place-value blocks to help you solve. Show your place-value blocks.

______ rocks

Visual Learning   A-Z Glossary

Visual Learning Bridge

You can show 47 and 26 with place-value blocks.

Find 47 + 26.

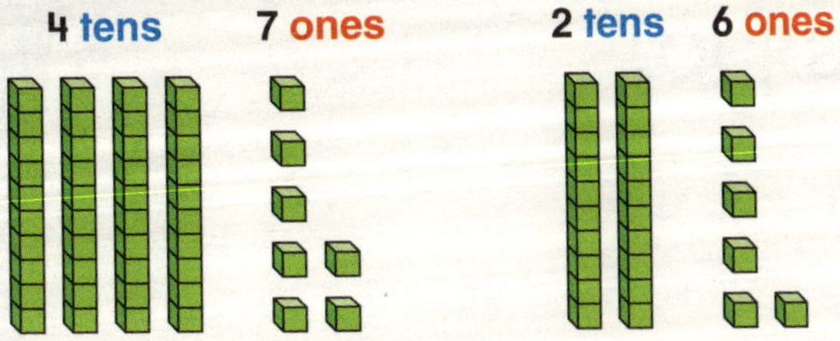

Join the tens and ones. **Regroup** if needed.

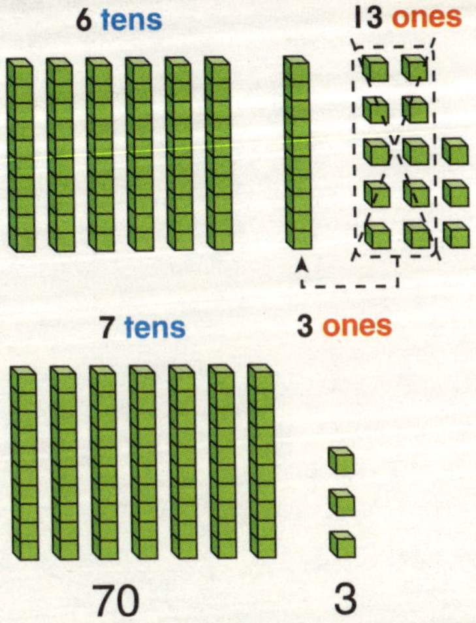

Regroup 13 ones as 1 ten and 3 ones.

So, 47 + 26 = 73.

Convince Me! When do you need to regroup when adding?

Guided Practice

Add. Use place-value blocks to find each sum. Regroup if needed.

1. 32 + 29 = ____

____ tens ____ ones

2. 24 + 52 = ____

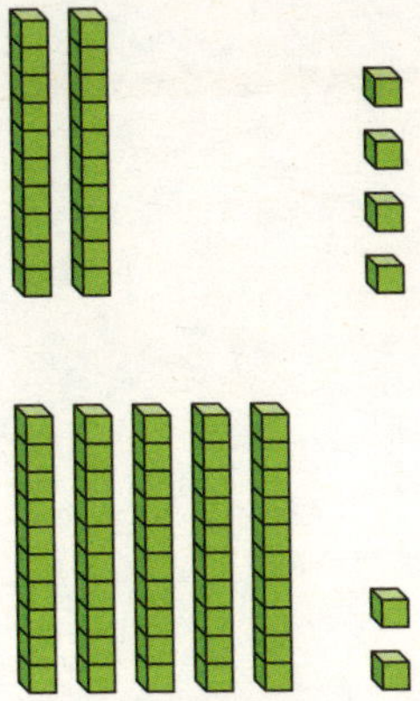

____ tens ____ ones

3. 15 + 38 = ____

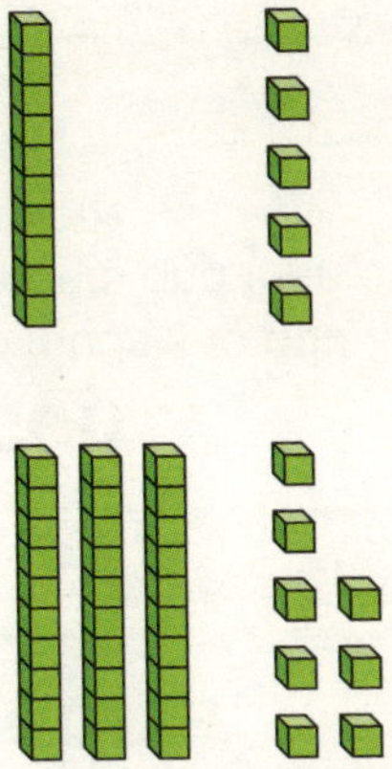

____ tens ____ ones

Name ____

Tools Assessment

Independent Practice

Add. Use place-value blocks to find each sum. Regroup if needed.

4. 36 + 29 = ______

5. 27 + 23 = ______

6. 59 + 13 = ______

7. 24 + 35 = ______

8. 58 + 25 = ______

9. 15 + 46 = ______

10. 75 + 19 = ______

11. 44 + 47 = ______

Higher Order Thinking Read the sum. Circle all of the number pairs in the box that match that sum.

12. Sum 22

10	4	18
12	15	14
20	21	13

13. Sum 55

25	30	14
18	14	45
15	21	10

14. Sum 83

30	45	30
56	19	64
27	29	20

Problem Solving
Solve the problems below. Show your work.

15. **Model** Chen counts 47 buttons. Then he counts 20 more buttons. How many buttons does Chen count in all?

_____ buttons

16. **enVision® STEM** There were 24 earthquakes in the U.S. one year. There were 28 earthquakes the next year. How many earthquakes were there in those two years?

_____ earthquakes

17. **Higher Order Thinking** Write an addition story about the desks and chairs in your classroom. Use pictures, numbers, or words.

18. **Assessment Practice** Do you have to regroup to find each sum? Choose Yes or No.

62 + 34 = ?	○ Yes	○ No
72 + 19 = ?	○ Yes	○ No
43 + 49 = ?	○ Yes	○ No
26 + 60 = ?	○ Yes	○ No

Name ______________________

Activity

Lesson 4-2

Continue to Add 2-Digit Numbers Using Models

I can ...
add numbers using place value and properties of operations.

I can also make sense of problems.

Solve & Share

Wendy picked 35 pears. Toni picked 49 pears. How many pears did they pick in all?

Use place-value blocks to help explain your work.

_____ pears

Visual Learning Bridge

Find 36 + 59.

One Way
Use quick drawings for the addends.

Join the tens and ones.
Regroup if needed.

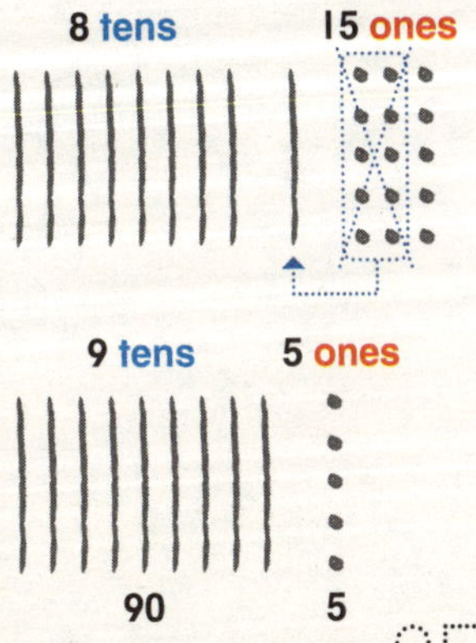

So, 36 + 59 = 95.

Another Way

  3 tens 6 ones
+ 5 tens 9 ones
  8 tens 15 ones

Think: 15 ones is 1 ten 5 ones.

8 tens 1 ten 5 ones
80 + 10 + 5 = 95

Convince Me! Ken adds 43 + 27. His sum is 60. Is he correct? Explain.

Guided Practice Add. Use place value. Draw blocks or use another way.

1. 12 + 23 = ____

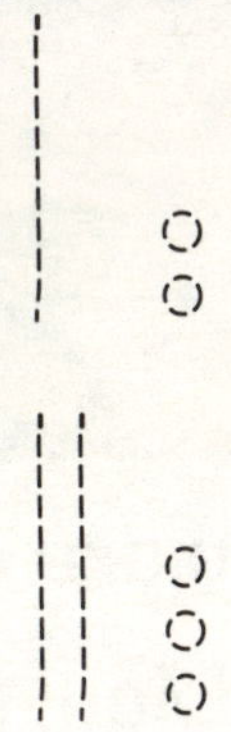

2. 18 + 42 = ____

  1 ten 8 ones
+ 4 tens 2 ones
  5 tens 10 ones

10 ones = 1 ten

5 tens + 1 ten =
6 tens

3. 33 + 48 = ____

Name ______________________________

Independent Practice

Add. Use place value. Draw blocks or use another way.

4. 18 + 24 = ____

5. 47 + 38 = ____

6. 26 + 47 = ____

7. 34 + 58 = ____

8. **Higher Order Thinking** Draw the second addend.

First Addend

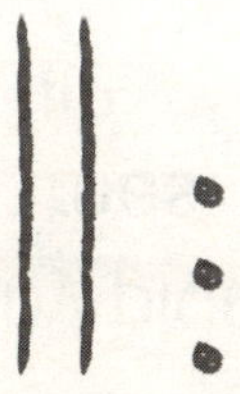

Second Addend

Sum

Problem Solving Solve each problem. Show your work.

9. Toby planted 28 trees. Juan planted 36 trees. How many trees did they plant in all?

_____ trees

10. **Make Sense** Jenny has 13 tennis balls. Sal had 16 tennis balls, but he gave 7 of them to Joe. How many tennis balls do Jenny and Sal have now?

_____ tennis balls

11. **Higher Order Thinking** Write an addition story using two 2-digit numbers. Then solve the problem for your story.

12. **Assessment Practice** Which is the same amount as 28 + 16? Choose all that apply.

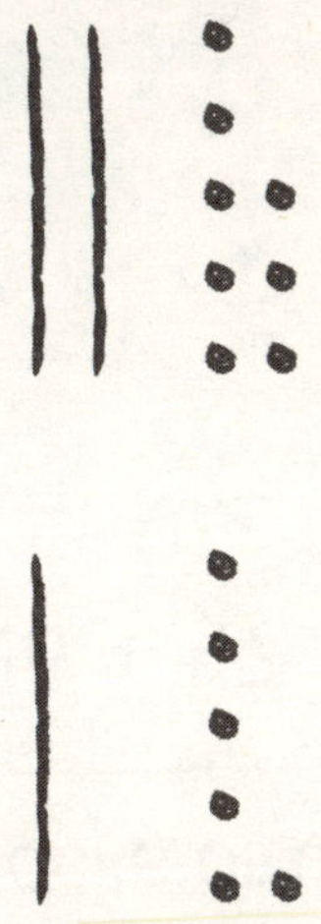

- ☐ 3 tens 1 ten 4 ones
- ☐ 30 + 10 + 4
- ☐ 34
- ☐ 44

Name ______________________________

Activity

Lesson 4-3
Add with Partial Sums

I can ...
add using place value and partial sums.

I can also look for patterns.

Solve & Share

Ms. Kim's class has 25 students. Mr. Will's class has 36 students. Both classes go on a field trip. How many students are on the trip?

Draw place-value blocks to help you solve the problem.

______ students

Visual Learning A-Z Glossary

Visual Learning Bridge

Find 57 + 28.

Tens	Ones
5	7
+ 2	8

Add the tens.

5 tens + 2 tens = 7 tens

Add the ones.

7 ones + 8 ones = 15 ones

Write the partial sums.

	Tens	Ones
	5	7
+	2	8
50 + 20 =	7	0
7 + 8 =	1	5

70 and 15 are the partial sums.

Then add the partial sums to find the sum.

	Tens	Ones
	5	7
+	2	8
50 + 20 =	7	0
7 + 8 =	1	5
Sum =	8	5

So, 57 + 28 = 85.

Convince Me! Can you add the ones first and then the tens when finding 57 + 28 using partial sums? Explain.

Guided Practice Add. Use partial sums. Draw blocks if you need to.

1. 24 + 13

	Tens	Ones
	2	4
+	1	3
20 + 10 =	3	0
4 + 3 =		7
Sum =		

2. 68 + 7

	Tens	Ones
	6	8
+		7
60 + 0 =		
8 + 7 =		
Sum =		

Name ______________________________

Independent Practice

Add. Use partial sums. Draw blocks if you need to.

3. 34 + 25

	Tens	Ones
	3	4
+	2	5
___ + ___ =		
___ + ___ =		
Sum =		

4. 68 + 18

	Tens	Ones
	6	8
+	1	8
___ + ___ =		
___ + ___ =		
Sum =		

5. 37 + 8

	Tens	Ones
	3	7
+		8
___ + ___ =		
___ + ___ =		
Sum =		

6. 52 + 38

	Tens	Ones
	5	2
+	3	8
___ + ___ =		
___ + ___ =		
Sum =		

7. 45 + 29

	Tens	Ones
	4	5
+	2	9
___ + ___ =		
___ + ___ =		
Sum =		

8. 28 + 39

	Tens	Ones
	2	8
+	3	9
___ + ___ =		
___ + ___ =		
Sum =		

Number Sense Write each missing tens or ones digit.

9. 23 + 1☐ = 37

10. 59 = ☐8 + 31

Problem Solving

Solve each problem. Show your work.

11. **Model** 34 students are on the playground. 17 students are in the gym. How many students are there in all?

_____ students

12. Sarah put 8 white roses in a vase. Then she added 7 red roses and 12 yellow roses to the vase. How many roses are in the vase now?

_____ roses

13. **Higher Order Thinking** Write each missing tens or ones digit. What strategy did you use?

12 + 3☐ = 50

24 + 3☐ = 60

35 + 3☐ = 70

14. **Assessment Practice** Which is the sum of 28 + 36? Use partial sums to solve.

Ⓐ 8

Ⓑ 12

Ⓒ 54

Ⓓ 64

Name ______________________________

Activity

Lesson 4-4

Add Using Mental Math and Partial Sums

I can ...
add numbers using place value and partial sums.

I can also make math arguments.

Solve & Share

Add 46 + 26.

Explain how you solved the problem.

____

____

____

Visual Learning   A-Z Glossary

Visual Learning Bridge

Find 56 + 17.

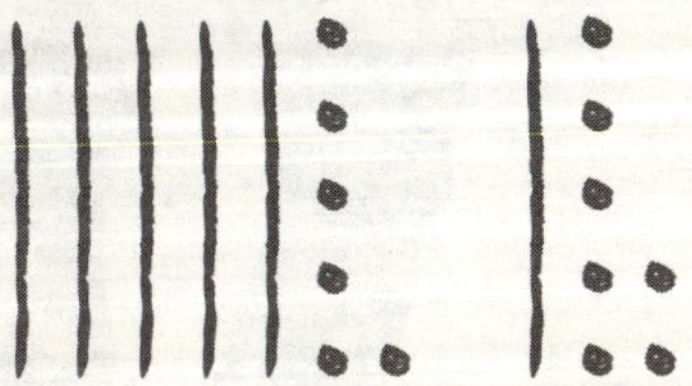

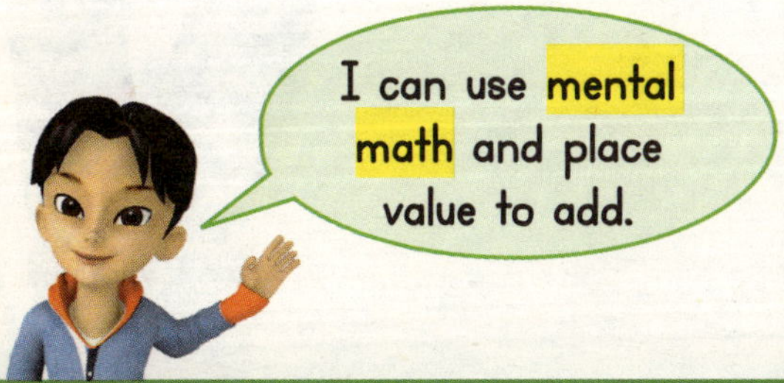

Mentally break apart the numbers using tens and ones.

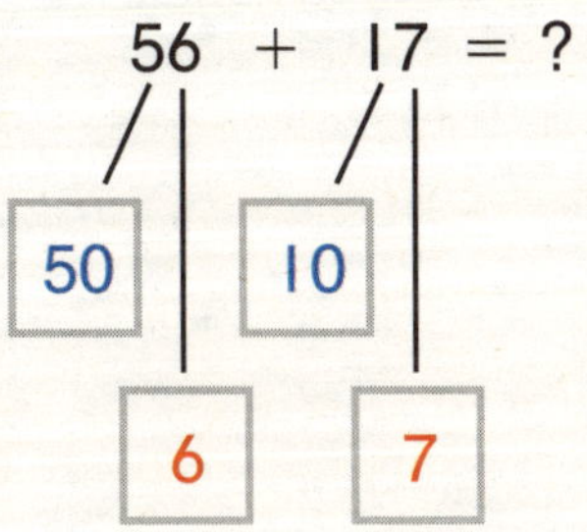

Find the partial sums.
Find the sum.

	Tens	Ones
	5	6
+	1	7
Tens:	6	0
Ones:	1	3
Sum:	7	3

So, 56 + 17 = 73.

Convince Me! Roger found 54 + 27. His sum was 71. Is he correct? Why or why not? Use partial sums to check.

Guided Practice

Write the addition problem. Use partial sums. Add any way you choose. Show your work.

1. 34 + 17

	Tens	Ones
+		
Tens:		
Ones:		
Sum:		

2. 52 + 31

	Tens	Ones
+		
Tens:		
Ones:		
Sum:		

3. 35 + 26

	Tens	Ones
+		
Tens:		
Ones:		
Sum:		

Name ______________________________

Tools Assessment

Independent Practice

Write the addition problem. Use partial sums. Add any way you choose. Show your work.

4. 15 + 28

	Tens	Ones
+		
Tens:		
Ones:		
Sum:		

5. 29 + 20

	Tens	Ones
+		
Tens:		
Ones:		
Sum:		

6. 63 + 29

	Tens	Ones
+		
Tens:		
Ones:		
Sum:		

7. 37 + 48

	Tens	Ones
+		
Tens:		
Ones:		
Sum:		

Add any way you choose. Show your work.

8. 67 + 17 = ____

9. 15 + 18 = ____

10. 43 + 49 = ____

11. 62 + 28 = ____

Number Sense Write the missing ones or tens digits.

12. 27 + 2☐ = 50

13. 3☐ + 16 = 48

14. ☐4 + 49 = 93

Problem Solving

Solve each problem. Show your work. Use drawings, if needed.

15. Amir plants 25 trees. Juan plants 27 trees. How many trees do they plant in all?

_____ trees

16. On Monday, Sasha puts 32 pennies in her bank. On Tuesday, she puts 57 more pennies in her bank. How many pennies does she put in her bank on both days?

_____ pennies

17. **Higher Order Thinking** Write an addition story using 2 two-digit numbers. Then solve the problem for your story.

18. **Assessment Practice** Find 52 + 39 using partial sums. Show how you solved the problem.

52 + 39 = _____

Name ______________________________

Activity

Lesson 4-5

Break Apart Numbers and Add Using Mental Math

I can ...
add within 100 using place-value strategies.

I can also reason about math.

Solve & Share

Monica has 24 crayons. Paul has 64 crayons. How many crayons do they have in all?

Use place-value blocks or draw a picture to explain your work.

_____ crayons

Visual Learning Bridge

Visual Learning · A-Z Glossary

Find 27 + 35.

One Way

Break apart the second addend to make a 10.

27 + 35 = ?

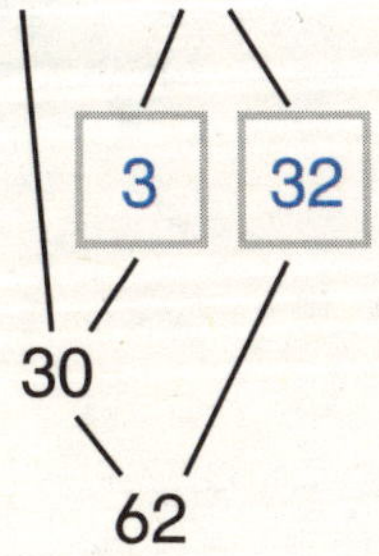

So, 27 + 35 = 62.

Another Way

Break apart the second addend into tens and ones.

27 + 35 = ?

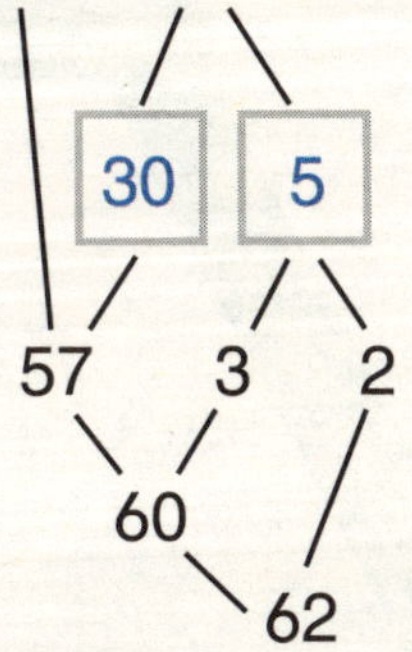

So, 27 + 35 = 62.

Convince Me! Explain one way you can break apart numbers to find 14 + 32.

Guided Practice Find each sum using mental math. Draw pictures of blocks if needed.

1. 17 + 52 = ____

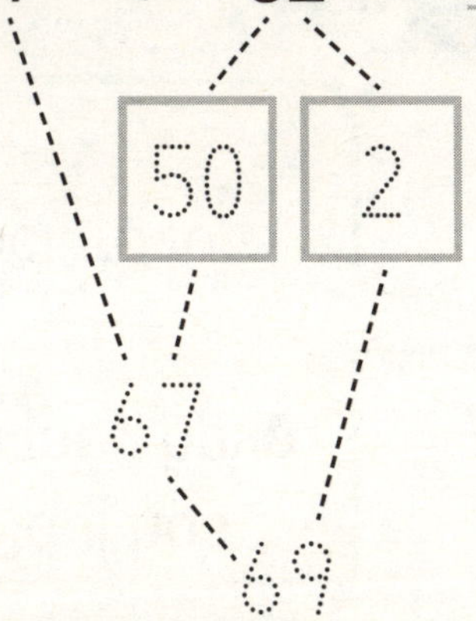

2. ____ = 69 + 23

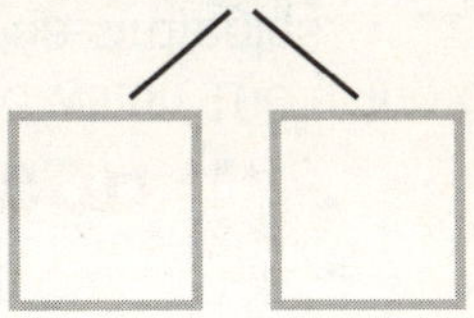

Name ____________________

Tools Assessment

Independent Practice

Find each sum using mental math. Draw pictures of blocks if needed.

3. 23 + 26 = ______ (26 broken into □ and □)

4. 9 + 42 = ______ (42 broken into □ and □)

5. ______ = 51 + 16 (16 broken into □ and □)

6. 56 + 15 = ______

7. ______ = 76 + 18

8. 33 + 49 = ______

Add tens and ones to solve.

9. **Algebra** One number makes both equations true. Find the missing number.

17 + □ = 28

□ + 28 = 39

Problem Solving

Generalize Solve each problem mentally. Show your work. Think about the steps you do every time you break apart numbers to add.

10. Billy puts 34 skateboard wheels in a pile. He puts 34 more wheels in another pile. How many wheels does Billy have in all?

_____ wheels

11. **enVision® STEM** A new office and house were built in a town. 24 windows are needed for the office. 18 windows are needed for the house. How many windows are needed in all?

_____ windows

12. **Higher Order Thinking** Write a story problem about 14 + 41. Then solve the problem.

$14 + 41 =$ _____

13. **Assessment Practice** Use mental math to find 15 + 12. Explain why the strategy works.

Name ______________________

Activity

Solve & Share

How can you use the hundred chart to help you find 57 – 23? Explain. Write an equation.

Lesson 5-1

Subtract Tens and Ones on a Hundred Chart

I can ...
use a hundred chart to subtract tens and ones.

I can also make math arguments.

1	2	3	4	5	6	7	8	9	10
11	12	13	14	15	16	17	18	19	20
21	22	23	24	25	26	27	28	29	30
31	32	33	34	35	36	37	38	39	40
41	42	43	44	45	46	47	48	49	50
51	52	53	54	55	56	57	58	59	60
61	62	63	64	65	66	67	68	69	70
71	72	73	74	75	76	77	78	79	80
81	82	83	84	85	86	87	88	89	90
91	92	93	94	95	96	97	98	99	100

_____ ◯ _____ = _____

Visual Learning | A-Z Glossary

Visual Learning Bridge

Find 43 – 28 using a hundred chart.

One Way Think: 43 – 28 = ?
Start at 43.
Count back 2 tens and 8 ones.
You land on 15.

11	12	13	14	15	16	17	18	19	20
21	22	23	24	25	26	27	28	29	30
31	32	33	34	35	36	37	38	39	40
41	42	43	44	45	46	47	48	49	50

So, 43 – 28 = 15.

Another Way Think: 28 + ? = 43
Start at 28. Count on to 43.

21	22	23	24	25	26	27	28	29	30
31	32	33	34	35	36	37	38	39	40
41	42	43	44	45	46	47	48	49	50

So, 28 + 15 = 43.

Convince Me! How can you use a hundred chart to find 60 – 18?

Guided Practice Subtract using the hundred chart. Draw arrows if you need to.

21	22	23	24	25	26	27	28	29	30
31	32	33	34	35	36	37	38	39	40
41	42	43	44	45	46	47	48	49	50
51	52	53	54	55	56	57	58	59	60
61	62	63	64	65	66	67	68	69	70

1. 69 – 36 = 33

2. 54 – 24 = ____

3. ____ = 65 – 34

4. 47 – 22 = ____

Name ______

Tools Assessment

Independent Practice

Subtract using the hundred chart. Draw arrows if you need to.

1	2	3	4	5	6	7	8	9	10
11	12	13	14	15	16	17	18	19	20
21	22	23	24	25	26	27	28	29	30
31	32	33	34	35	36	37	38	39	40
41	42	43	44	45	46	47	48	49	50
51	52	53	54	55	56	57	58	59	60
61	62	63	64	65	66	67	68	69	70
71	72	73	74	75	76	77	78	79	80
81	82	83	84	85	86	87	88	89	90
91	92	93	94	95	96	97	98	99	100

5. 54 – 7 = ______

6. ______ = 96 – 63

7. 45 – 22 = ______

8. 82 – 61 = ______

9. 65 – 21 = ______

10. ______ = 79 – 47

11. 84 – 6 = ______

Algebra Write the digit that makes each equation true.

12. 73 – ☐2 = 41

5☐ – 32 = 26

13. 46 – ☐1 = 15

78 – 36 = ☐2

14. 53 – ☐2 = 31

99 – ☐3 = 16

Problem Solving **Use Tools** Use the hundred chart to solve the problems below.

41	42	43	44	45	46	47	48	49	50
51	52	53	54	55	56	57	58	59	60
61	62	63	64	65	66	67	68	69	70
71	72	73	74	75	76	77	78	79	80
81	82	83	84	85	86	87	88	89	90
91	92	93	94	95	96	97	98	99	100

15. Darren's puzzle has 98 pieces. Darren fits 55 pieces together. How many more pieces does Darren still need to fit to complete the puzzle?

____ ◯ ____ = ____ pieces

16. A test has 86 questions. Glenda needs to answer 23 more questions to finish the test. How many test questions has Glenda answered already?

____ questions

17. **Higher Order Thinking** Chris wants to subtract 76 – 42. Write the steps he can take to subtract 42 from 76 on the hundred chart.

____

____

____

____

18. **Assessment Practice** Which has a difference of 26? Choose all that apply.

- ☐ 56 – 30
- ☐ 69 – 43
- ☐ 75 – 49
- ☐ 92 – 76

Name ____________________

Activity

Lesson 5-2

Count Back to Subtract on an Open Number Line

I can ...
use an open number line to subtract tens and ones.

I can also model with math.

Solve & Share

Jeremy had 56 bug stickers.
He gave 24 stickers to Eric.
How many bug stickers does Jeremy have left?
Use the open number line below to show your work.

____ ◯ ____ = ____

Visual Learning Bridge

Visual Learning   A-Z Glossary

Find 68 – 23.

One Way

23 is 2 tens and 3 ones.
So, count back 2 tens from 68.
58, 48
Then, count back 3 ones from 48.
47, 46, 45

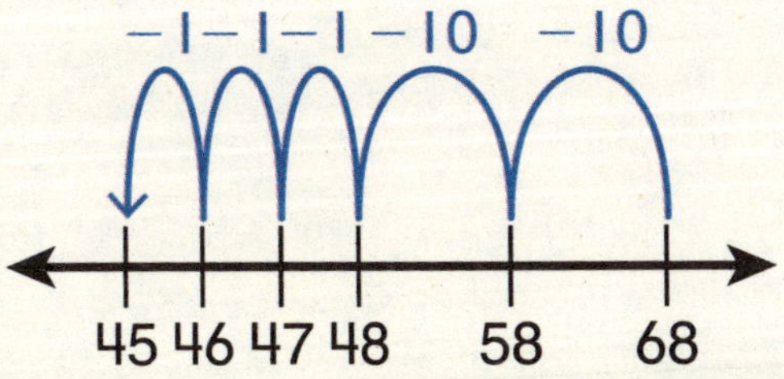

Another Way

You can subtract 68 – **20** = 48,
then 48 – **3** = 45.

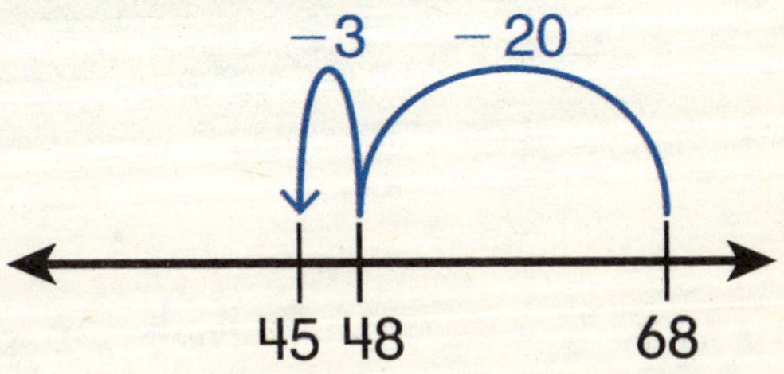

So, 68 – 23 = 45.

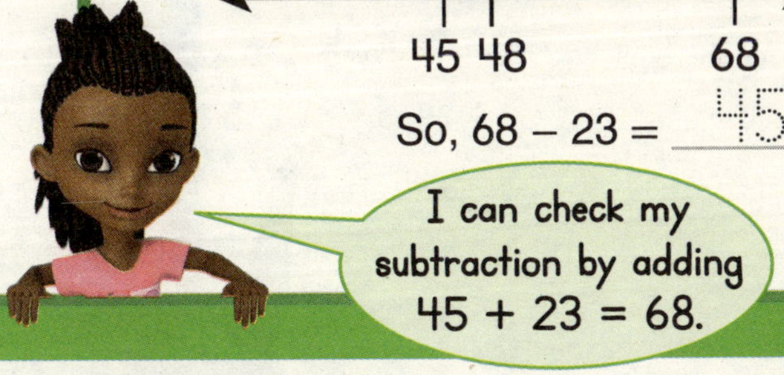

Convince Me! How can the open number line help you keep track as you count back?

☆ **Guided Practice** ☆ Use an open number line to find each difference.

1. 28 – 24 = ____

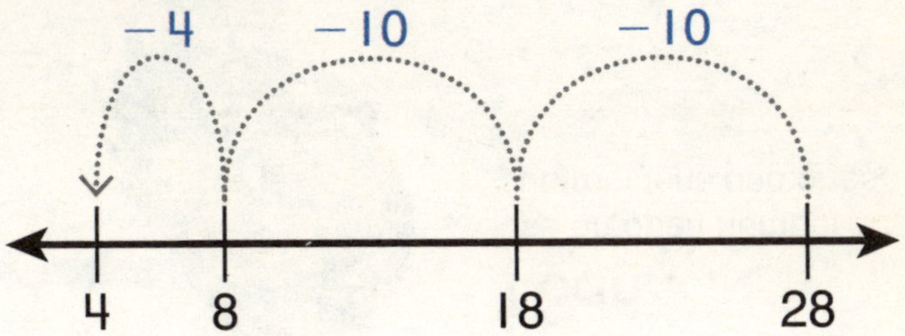

2. 50 – 35 = ____

Name ______________________________

Tools Assessment

Independent Practice

Use an open number line to find each difference.

3. 45 − 13 = ____

4. 63 − 22 = ____

5. 78 − 46 = ____

6. 92 − 37 = ____

7. 80 − 44 = ?

____ − ____ = ____

8. **Number Sense** How many tens and ones will you count back to solve this problem: 56 − 38 = ? Solve the problem.

____ tens ____ ones

____ − ____ = ____

Problem Solving

Use an open number line to solve each problem.

9. Use Tools There are 47 raffle tickets to sell for the fair. Ms. Brown's class sells 23 raffle tickets. How many raffle tickets are left to sell?

_____ raffle tickets

10. Use Tools Ethan counts 78 carrots. He sells 35 carrots at the farmers market. How many carrots does Ethan have left?

_____ carrots

11. Higher Order Thinking Show two different ways to find 63 − 25 using the open number lines.

63 − 25 = _____

12. Assessment Practice Jen solved a subtraction problem using the open number line shown. Write the equation that her work below shows.

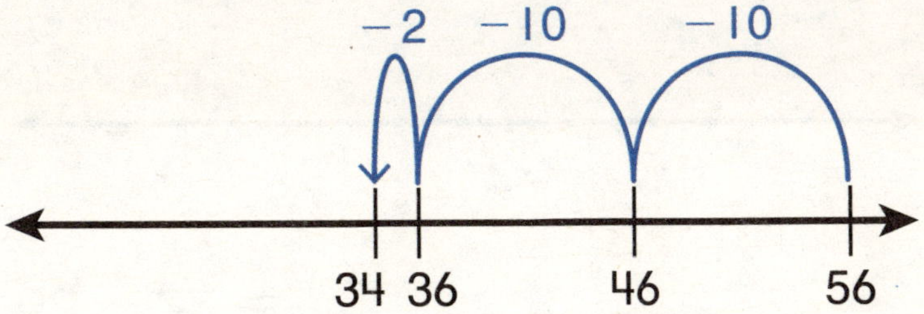

_____ − _____ = _____

Name ____________________

Solve & Share

There are 50 children at the park. 28 are boys and the rest are girls. How many girls are at the park?

Use the open number line to solve. Show your work.

Activity

Lesson 5-3

Add Up to Subtract Using an Open Number Line

I can ... add up to subtract using an open number line.

I can also reason about math.

____ ◯ ____ = ____

Visual Learning Bridge

Find 57 – 28.

You can add 2 to get to 30.

Then add 10, and 10 again, to get to 50.

Then add 7 to land on 57.

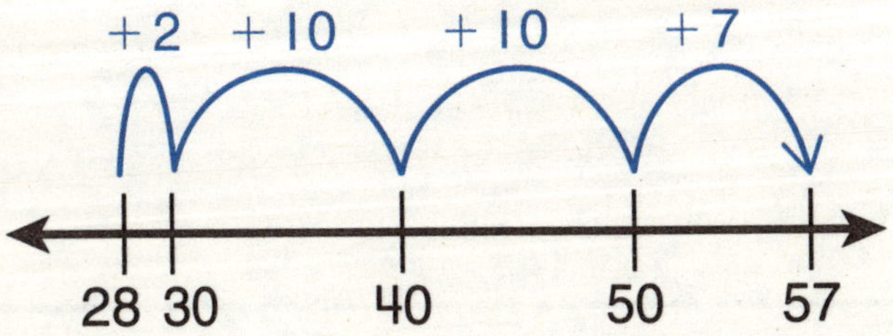

Add the tens and ones.

2 + 10 + 10 + 7 = 29

So, 57 – 28 = 29.

Convince Me! How can you add up to find 42 – 17?

Guided Practice Add up to find each difference. Use an open number line.

1. 45 – 27 = 18

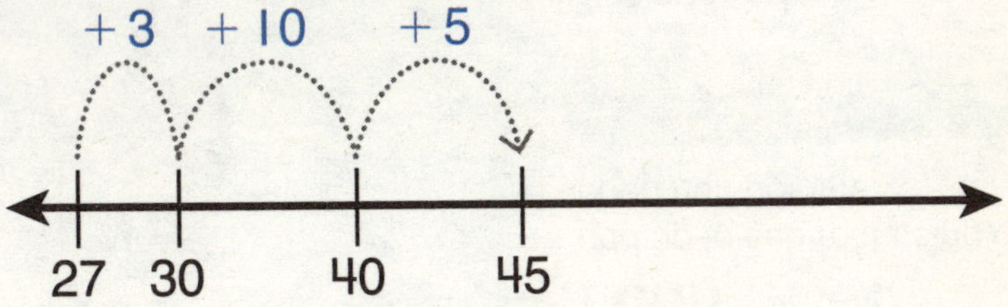

2. 66 – 39 = ____

Name ______________________

Tools Assessment

Independent Practice

Add up to find each difference.
Use an open number line.

3. 41 − 19 = ____

4. 63 − 34 = ____

5. 83 − 58 = ____

6. 74 − 46 = ____

7. 72 − 34 = ____

8. **enVision® STEM** Rob had 34 snowballs. Some melted and now he has 18 snowballs. How many snowballs melted?

____ ◯ ____ = ____

Problem Solving

Add up to solve each problem. Use an open number line. Write the equations.

9. Be Precise Dino has 41 crayons. He gives 23 crayons to Bridget, and 7 crayons to Dan. How many crayons does Dino have left? Solve using two steps.

Step 1: ____ ◯ ____ = ____

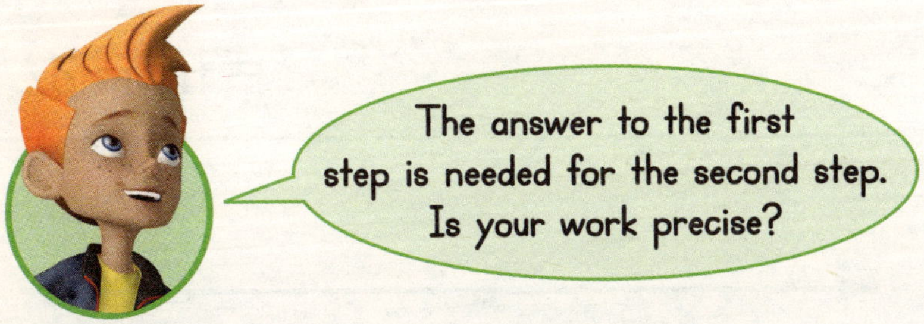

Step 2: ____ ◯ ____ = ____

10. Higher Order Thinking Show two different ways to add up to find 72 – 35.

1. ____ – ____ = ____

11. Assessment Practice Find 46 – 25. Show your work on the open number line and then write an equation.

____ ◯ ____ = ____

Name ______________________

Activity

Lesson 5-4

Break Apart Numbers to Subtract

Solve & Share

Use any strategy to find 42 – 7. Use pictures, words, or numbers to explain.

I can ...
break apart 1-digit numbers to help me subtract mentally.

I can also make math arguments.

42 – 7 = ____

Visual Learning A-Z Glossary

Visual Learning Bridge

33 – 6 = ?

You can break apart the number you are subtracting to find the difference.

6 → 1 + 5

6 → 2 + 4

6 → 3 + 3

33 – 6 = ___ ?

6 → 3, 3

11	12	13	14	15	16	17	18	19	20
21	22	23	24	25	26	27	28	29	30
31	32	33	34	35	36	37	38	39	40

33 – 6 = 27

Convince Me! Look at the problem above. Why wasn't the 6 broken apart into 1 + 5 to find 33 – 6?

Guided Practice Subtract. Break apart the number you are subtracting. Show your work.

1. 43 – 9 = ___

2. ___ = 24 – 6

11	12	13	14	15	16	17	18	19	20
21	22	23	24	25	26	27	28	29	30
31	32	33	34	35	36	37	38	39	40
41	42	43	44	45	46	47	48	49	50

Name ______

Independent Practice

Subtract. Break apart the number you are subtracting. Show your work. Use a hundred chart if needed.

3. 35 − 8 = ____

4. 41 − 5 = ____

5. ____ = 82 − 7

6. 53 − 7 = ____

7. 97 − 8 = ____

8. 64 − 9 = ____

9. 86 − 8 = ____

10. ____ = 32 − 9

11. 93 − 6 = ____

12. **Algebra** One number makes both equations true. Find the missing number.

48 + ☐ = 56   56 − ☐ = 48

The missing number is ____.

Think about how addition and subtraction are related.

Problem Solving

Solve each problem. Show your work.

13. **Explain** Karen has 7 pencils. Karen's teacher has 45 pencils. How many fewer pencils does Karen have than her teacher? Explain how you solved the problem.

____

____

____

_____ fewer pencils

14. **Higher Order Thinking** Write a story problem about 63 – 8. Then solve.

$63 - 8 =$ _____

15. Duane has 24 seashells. He gives 9 shells to his cousin Rob. How many seashells does Duane have now?

Ⓐ 16 Ⓒ 14

Ⓑ 15 Ⓓ 13

16. **Assessment Practice** Find 86 – 7. Show your work.

$86 - 7 =$ _____

Name ______________________________

Activity

Lesson 5-5
Subtract Using Compensation

Solve & Share

Yuri wants to use mental math to find 86 – 29. Show how Yuri could find the difference. Explain how she could use mental math.

I can ...

make numbers that are easier to subtract, then use mental math to find the difference.

I can also use repeated reasoning.

Visual Learning | A-Z Glossary

Visual Learning Bridge

43 − 18 = ?

You can use compensation to make numbers that are easier to subtract.

One Way
Change both addends by adding or subtracting the same amount. Then subtract using mental math.

43 − 18 = ?
↓+2 ↓+2
45 − 20 = 25

So, 43 − 18 = 25.

Another Way
Add 2 to 18.
Then subtract using mental math.
Then add 2 to find the answer.

43 − 18 = ?
↓+2
43 − 20 = 23
↓+2
So, 43 − 18 = 25.

Convince Me! Marc says to find 61 − 13, it's easier to subtract 10 instead of 13. He says if you subtract 3 from 13 to get 10, you must subtract 3 more from your answer. Do you agree? Explain.

Guided Practice Use compensation to make numbers that are easier to subtract. Then solve. Show your work.

1. 52 − 8 = ____
↓+2 ↓+2
54 − 10 = 44

2. 76 − 27 = ____
↓☐ ↓☐
____ − ____ = ____

3. 52 − 15 = ____
↓+5
52 − 20 = 32 → 37
+5

4. 93 − 39 = ____
↓☐
____ ○ ____ = ____ → 54
☐

Name ______________________

Tools Assessment

Independent Practice Use compensation to make numbers that are easier to subtract. Then solve. Show your work.

5. 73 − 9 = _____

6. 35 − 16 = _____

7. 43 − 28 = _____

8. 51 − 27 = _____

9. 74 − 35 = _____

10. 99 − 21 = _____

11. **Higher Order Thinking** Yoshi says that to find 91 − 32, he can subtract 2 from both numbers. Then he can subtract using mental math. He says the answer is 59. Do you agree? Explain.

Problem Solving

Solve each problem. Show your thinking.

12. **Make Sense** There were some buttons in a jar. Mrs. Kim puts 19 more buttons in the same jar. Now there are 45 buttons in the jar. How many buttons were in the jar to begin with?

_____ buttons

13. Romi has 42 cards. Lisa has 75 cards. How many more cards does Lisa have than Romi?

_____ more cards

14. **Higher Order Thinking** Greg found 72 – 24. First he subtracted 20 because he thinks it is easier. Use words and numbers to explain how Greg could have found the difference.

15. **Assessment Practice** Use the numbers on the cards. Write the missing numbers to solve the problem.

2 | 25 | 30 | 55

53 – 28 = _____

+ 2 + ☐

_____ – _____ = _____

Name ____________________

Solve & Share

How can you use tens and ones to find 23 – 6? Use place-value blocks to help you. Show your work.

____ – ____ = ____

Lesson 6-1

Subtract 1-Digit Numbers Using Models

I can ...
use place value and models to subtract 1-digit numbers.

I can also use math tools correctly.

Visual Learning A-Z Glossary

Visual Learning Bridge

Find 34 – 6. Use place-value blocks.

Show 34 with tens and ones.

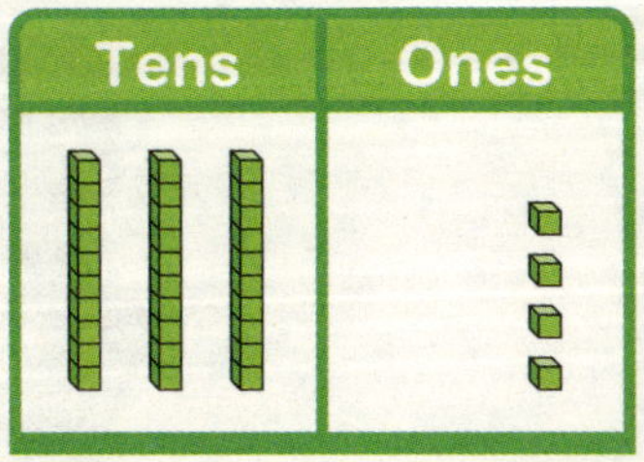

3 tens   4 ones

One Way
Take away 4 ones.
Regroup 1 ten as 10 ones.
Take away 2 more ones.

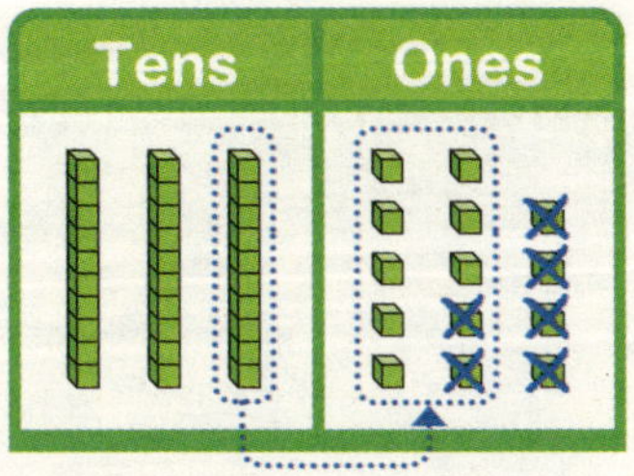

2 tens   8 ones

Another Way
Regroup 1 ten as 10 ones first.
Then take away 6 ones.

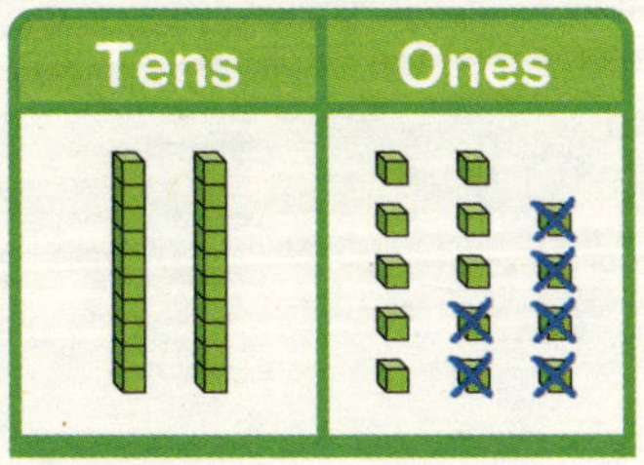

2 tens   8 ones

Cross out 6 ones. Now there are 2 tens and 8 ones left. This shows the difference.

So, 34 – 6 = 28.

Convince Me! In the first example above, why were 4 ones taken away first?

Guided Practice

Subtract. Use place-value blocks. Draw blocks to show your work.

1. 63 – 2 = ____

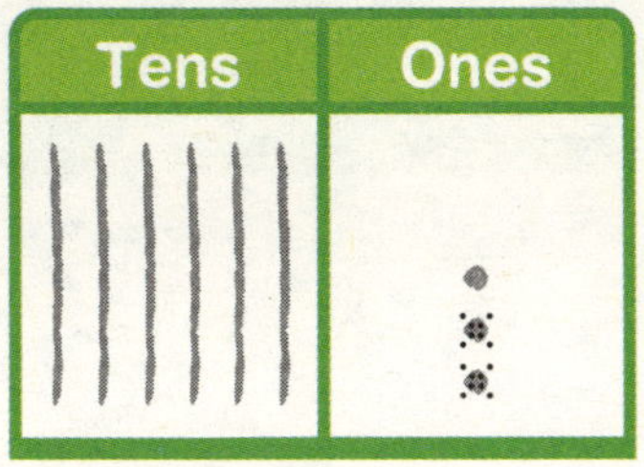

2. 44 – 9 = ____

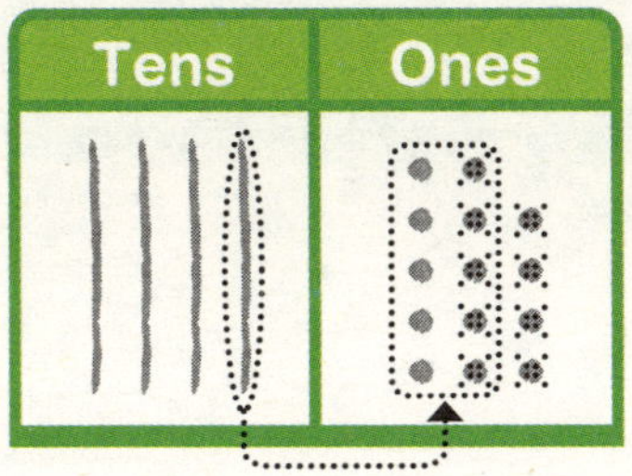

3. 32 – 8 = ____

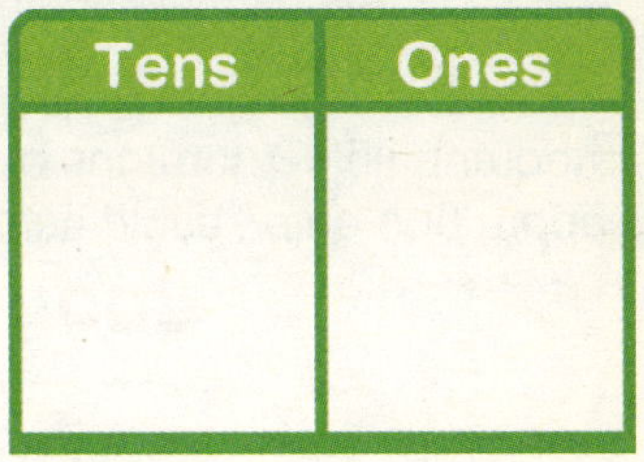

Name ____________________

Tools Assessment

Independent Practice

Subtract. Use place-value blocks. Draw blocks to show your work.

4. 29 − 1 = ____

Tens	Ones

5. 50 − 7 = ____

Tens	Ones

6. 61 − 4 = ____

Tens	Ones

7. 43 − 5 = ____

Tens	Ones

8. 86 − 9 = ____

Tens	Ones

9. 39 − 3 = ____

Tens	Ones

10. 56 − 8 = ____

Tens	Ones

11. 21 − 6 = ____

Tens	Ones

12. **Higher Order Thinking** Which one-digit numbers can you subtract from 74 without first regrouping? Explain how you know.

____

____

____

Problem Solving

Solve each problem below.

13. How can place-value blocks help you find 66 – 8? Explain.

____

____

____

____

14. **Make Sense** Kate has 45 marbles. She gives 3 marbles to her brother. How many marbles does Kate have now?

_____ marbles

15. **Higher Order Thinking** Sammie has 9 fewer rings than Emilio.
Sammie has 7 more rings than Sara.
Emilio has 34 rings.
Complete the sentences below.
Draw a picture to explain your work.

Sammie has _____ rings. Sara has _____ rings.

16. **Assessment Practice** Draw place-value blocks to find 34 – 8. Which is the difference?

Tens	Ones

Ⓐ 22

Ⓑ 26

Ⓒ 28

Ⓓ 46

Name ______________________

Activity

Lesson 6-2

Subtract 2-Digit Numbers Using Models

I can ...
use place value and models to subtract 2-digit numbers.

I can also model with math.

Solve & Share

You have 42 pipe cleaners.
You use 19 of the pipe cleaners.
How many pipe cleaners do you have now?

Use place-value blocks to help you solve.
Draw place-value blocks to show your work.

_____ pipe cleaners

Visual Learning A-Z Glossary

Visual Learning Bridge

Find 43 – 24. Use place-value blocks.

One Way
Take away 2 tens 3 ones.

Regroup 1 ten as 10 ones.
Take away 1 more.

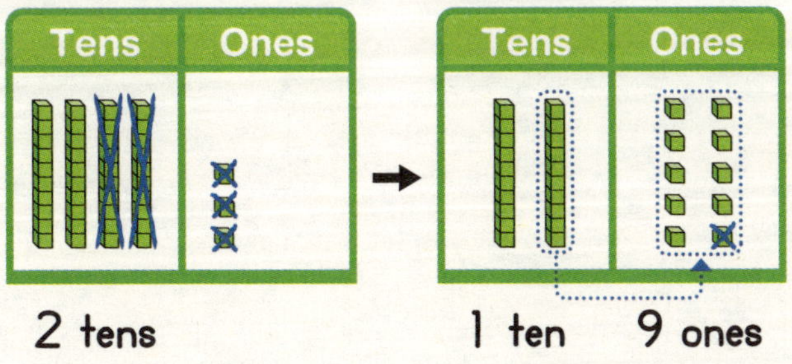

So, 43 – 24 = 19.

Another Way
Take away 2 tens.

Regroup 1 ten as 10 ones.
Take away 4 ones.

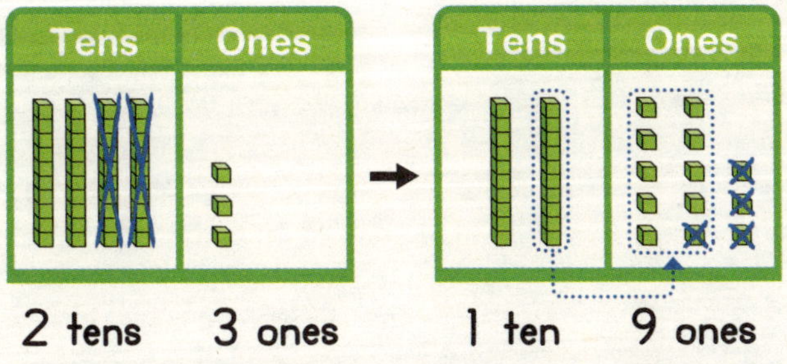

So, 43 – 24 = 19.

Convince Me! How are the two ways shown above alike? How are they different?

Guided Practice Subtract. Use place-value blocks. Draw blocks to show your work.

1. 52 – 13 = ____

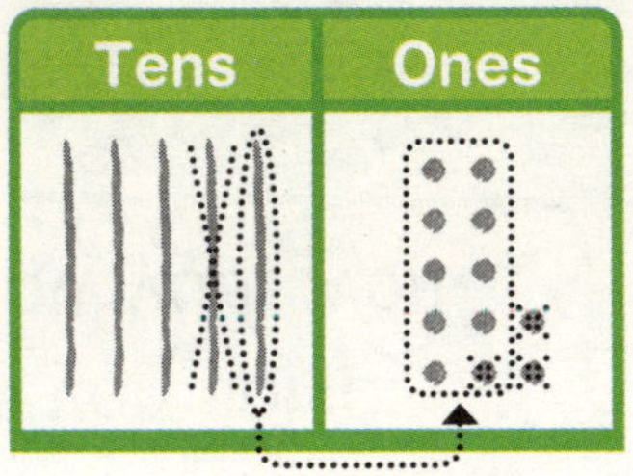

2. 46 – 25 = ____

Tens	Ones

3. 65 – 37 = ____

Tens	Ones

Name ______________________________

Tools Assessment

Independent Practice

Subtract. Use place-value blocks. Draw blocks to show your work.

4. 56 – 31 = ____

Tens	Ones

5. 63 – 24 = ____

Tens	Ones

6. 72 – 46 = ____

Tens	Ones

7. 57 – 15 = ____

Tens	Ones

8. 25 – 19 = ____

Tens	Ones

9. 84 – 27 = ____

Tens	Ones

10. 41 – 13 = ____

Tens	Ones

11. 90 – 38 = ____

Tens	Ones

12. **Algebra** Write numbers to complete the equations. Draw pictures to help if needed.

37 – 18 = ☐

46 – ☐ = 18

☐ – 17 = 16

13. **Number Sense** Do these models show the same value? Explain.

____

____

____

____

Problem Solving

Solve each problem.

14. Model Anita has $63. She spends $24 and saves the rest. How much does Anita save?

Tens	Ones

$______

15. Higher Order Thinking Write a subtraction story about 36 – 17. Explain how to solve the problem.

16. Assessment Practice Draw place-value blocks to find 70 – 11. Which is the difference?

Tens	Ones

Ⓐ 59

Ⓑ 49

Ⓒ 47

Ⓓ 11

Name ______________________________

Activity

Lesson 6-3

Subtract Using Partial Differences

I can ...

subtract using place value and partial differences.

I can also reason about math.

Solve & Share

Ari has 72 stickers. He puts 25 of his stickers in a scrapbook. How many stickers are left?

Draw place-value blocks to help you solve the problem.

Visual Learning · A-Z Glossary

Visual Learning Bridge

Find 64 – 36.
You can use place-value blocks to subtract and record **partial differences**.

What You Show

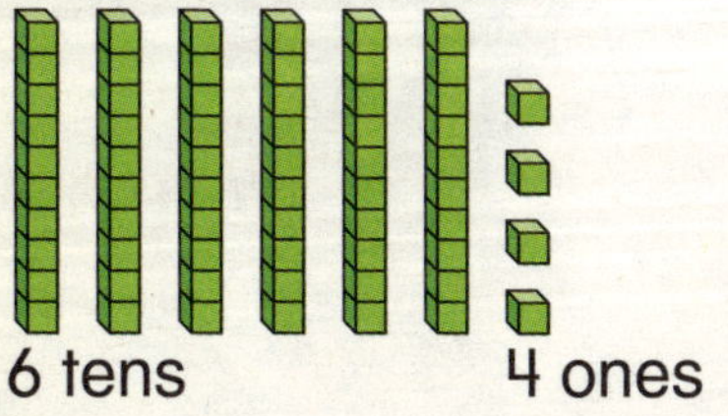

You can subtract 3 tens from 6 tens.

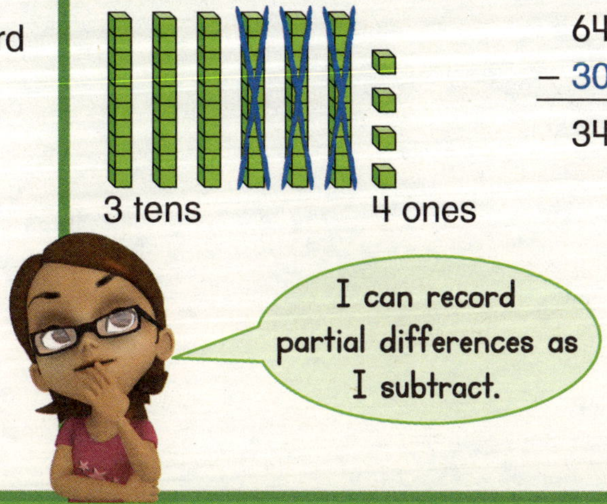

64
– 30
34

Subtract 6 ones.
First, subtract 4 ones to make a 10.

Regroup 1 ten as 10 ones.
Then subtract 2 ones.

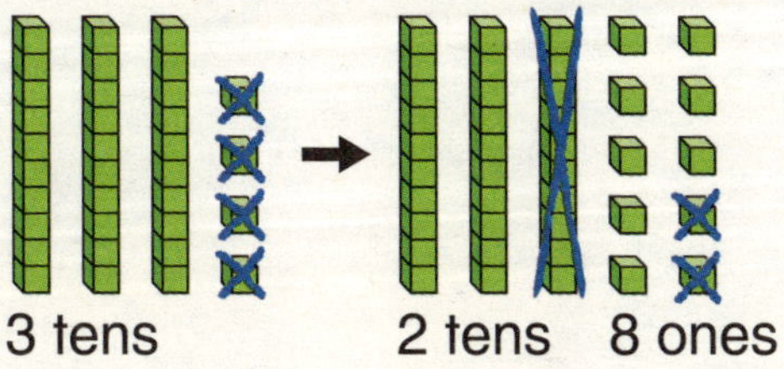

64
– 30
34
– 4
30
– 2
28

So, 64 – 36 = 28.

Convince Me! The example above shows one way to find 64 – 36 using partial differences. Could you begin by subtracting the ones instead of the tens? Explain.

Guided Practice Subtract. Use place-value blocks to find partial differences. Record your work.

1. 34 – 15 = ____

34
– 10 Subtract 1 ten.
24
– 4 Subtract 4 ones.
20
– 1 Subtract 1.

2. 63 – 48 = ____

63
– 3 Subtract 3 ones.
60
– 5 Subtract 5 ones.
55
– 40 Subtract 4 tens.

Name ______

Tools Assessment

Independent Practice

Subtract. Use place-value blocks to find partial differences. Record your work.

3. 52 − 36 = ____

4. 94 − 54 = ____

5. 41 − 25 = ____

6. 33 − 28 = ____

7. 65 − 42 = ____

8. 70 − 48 = ____

9. 96 − 37 = ____

10. 87 − 45 = ____

Solve. Draw a model to help.

11. **Higher Order Thinking** Tia's basketball team scored 61 points. They won by 23 points. How many points did the other team score?

____ points

Problem Solving Solve each problem.

12. **Model** Don has 72 marbles. Josie has 56 marbles. How many more marbles does Don have than Josie?

_____ more marbles

13. **Higher Order Thinking** Write a subtraction story using two 2-digit numbers. Then solve the problem in your story.

14. **Assessment Practice** Which numbers will complete this partial differences problem for 44 − 17?

Choose all that apply.

$$\begin{array}{r} 44 \\ -\ 10 \\ \hline ? \\ -\ 4 \\ \hline ? \\ -\ 3 \\ \hline 27 \end{array}$$

- ☐ 20
- ☐ 30
- ☐ 31
- ☐ 34

Name ____________________

Solve & Share

Show two different ways to find 53 – 28.

Activity

Lesson 6-4

Continue to Subtract Using Partial Differences

I can ...
use partial differences and mentally break apart the number I am subtracting.

I can also make sense of problems.

Visual Learning Bridge

Find 81 – 27.

You know how to count back on a number line to subtract.

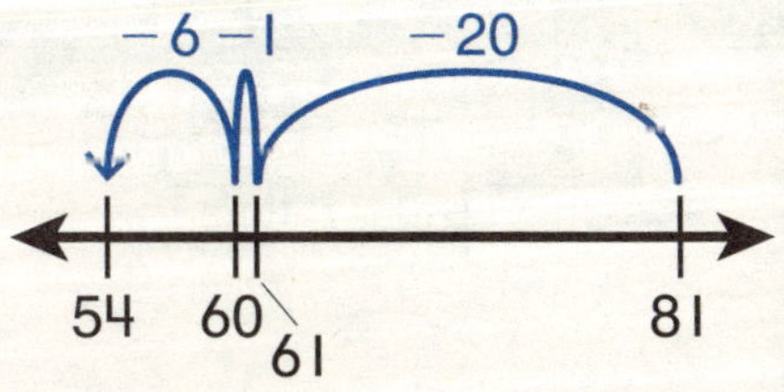

You can also mentally break apart the number you are subtracting.

81 – 27 = ?

27 → 20 and 7

7 → 1 and 6

You can record partial differences.

$$\begin{array}{r} 81 \\ -\ 20 \\ \hline 61 \\ -\ 1 \\ \hline 60 \\ -\ 6 \\ \hline 54 \end{array}$$

So, 81 – 27 = 54.

Convince Me! Find 73 – 45. Andy says he can subtract 3, then 2, and then 40 to find the difference. Do you agree? Explain.

Guided Practice

Subtract. Use partial differences. Break apart the number you are subtracting. Show your work.

1. 54 – 26 = ____

26 → 20 and 6

6 → 4 and ☐

$$\begin{array}{r} 54 \\ -\ 20 \\ \hline \end{array}$$

2. 43 – 18 = ____

18 → ☐ and ☐

☐ → ☐ and ☐

Name ______________________________

Tools Assessment

Independent Practice Subtract. Use partial differences. Break apart the number you are subtracting. Show your work.

3. _____ = 32 − 13

4. 74 − 28 = _____

5. _____ = 61 − 47

6. 84 − 46 = _____

7. 59 − 17 = _____

8. _____ = 95 − 38

9. **Higher Order Thinking** Tina found 53 − 27 by breaking apart 27 into 23 and 4. Does Tina's way work?

Show another way you could break apart 27 to find 53 − 27. Then find the difference.

Problem Solving

Solve each problem. Show your work.

10. **enVision® STEM** Kate had 32 ice cubes. She put 14 of them in the sun and they melted. How many ice cubes does Kate have now?

_____ ice cubes

11. **Make Sense** Mark has 27 stamps. Sam has 82 stamps. Lena has 42 stamps. How many more stamps does Sam have than Mark?

_____ more stamps

12. **Higher Order Thinking** Allison found $51 - 34$ using partial differences. She broke apart 34 into $31 + 3$.

Write equations to show how Allison could have found the difference.

13. **Assessment Practice** Can you use the equations to find $63 - 45$? Choose Yes or No.

$63 - 3 = 60$ ○ Yes ○ No
$60 - 2 = 58$
$58 - 40 = 18$

$63 - 40 = 23$ ○ Yes ○ No
$23 - 5 = 18$

$45 - 10 = 35$ ○ Yes ○ No
$35 - 5 = 30$

Name ______________________________

Activity

Lesson 7-1

Represent Addition and Subtraction Problems

I can ...
model problems using equations with unknowns in any position.

I can also model with math.

Solve & Share

Jenn has some red cubes and 11 blue cubes. She has 24 red and blue cubes in all.

She says the problem can be shown with the equation below.

$$? + 11 = 24$$

Draw what the ? represents. Explain your answer.

Visual Learning · A-Z Glossary

Visual Learning Bridge

Robert has 27 toy robots. He buys some more. Now he has 58 robots. How many robots did Robert buy?

You can show the problem with an equation.

$27 + ? = 58$

You can solve the problem by adding on from 27 until you get to 58.

$27 + 10 = 37$
$37 + 10 = 47$
$47 + 10 = 57$
$57 + 1 = 58$

$10 + 10 + 10 + 1 = 31$

So, $27 + 31 = 58$.

Robert bought 31 robots.

You can subtract to solve the problem.

$58 - 27$

20 7

$58 - 20 = 38$
$38 - 7 = 31$

You can check by adding.

$31 + 27 = 58$

Robert bought 31 robots.

Convince Me! Could you show Robert's robot problem with the equation below? Explain.

$58 = 27 + ?$

Guided Practice Write an equation with a ? for the unknown to model the problem. Then solve. Show your work.

1. Mary has some game tickets. She gives away 14 tickets and now has 17 tickets left. How many tickets did she have at first?

   Equation: $? - 14 = 17$ ______ tickets

2. Tamara has \$25. She earns \$34 more by working. How much money does she have now?

   Equation: ______ \$ ______

Name ______________________________

Tools Assessment

Independent Practice

Write an equation with a ? for the unknown to model the problem. Then solve. Show your work.

3. Erin has 32 books on her bookshelf. She gives some to friends and now has 19 books left. How many books did she give away?

Equation: ______________________

______ books

4. A store sells 38 men's bikes and 47 women's bikes. How many bikes did the store sell in all?

Equation: ______________________

______ bikes

5. **enVision® STEM** A field has 25 trees in it. 14 trees are new and the rest are old. How many trees are old? Write two different equations that represent the problem. Then solve.

Equation: ______________________

Equation: ______________________

______ old trees

6. **Number Sense** Harry buys 22 fish. He has a round fish bowl and a rectangular fish tank. How could he place the fish in the bowl and tank?

Equation: ______________________

______ fish in the bowl ______ fish in the tank

Problem Solving

Write an equation with a ? for the unknown to model the problem. Then solve. Show your work.

7. **Model** Rodney collects 17 leaves and Sheila collects 23 leaves. How many more leaves does Sheila collect than Rodney?

Equation: ______________

______ more leaves

8. **Model** Jun swims 18 laps and Mara swims 25 laps. How many fewer laps did Jun swim than Mara?

Equation: ______________

______ fewer laps

9. **Higher Order Thinking** Jim has 44 roses. 14 are white and the rest are red. How many are red? Write two different equations to model the problem. Then solve.

Equation: ______________

Equation: ______________

______ red roses

10. **Assessment Practice** Some wolves howl in the woods. 12 wolves join them. Now 30 wolves howl. How many wolves howled at first?

Which equation models the problem? Choose all that apply.

- ☐ ? + 12 = 30
- ☐ 30 = 12 + ?
- ☐ 30 + 12 = ?
- ☐ 30 = ? + 12

Name ______________________________

Activity

Lesson 7-2

Mixed Practice: Solve Addition and Subtraction Problems

Solve & Share

Aiden has 27 fewer crayons this week than last week. Last week he had 56 crayons. How many crayons does Aiden have this week? Show your work.

I can ...
use drawings and equations to make sense of the words in problems.

I can also make sense of problems.

______ crayons

Visual Learning A-Z Glossary

Visual Learning Bridge

Sally has 28 fewer blocks than Nigel.
Sally has 26 blocks.
How many blocks does Nigel have?

Let's think about who has fewer blocks and who has more blocks.

A bar diagram can help you think about the problem.

Nigel's blocks

?	
26	28
Sally's blocks	28 blocks fewer

26 + 28 = ?

Sally has 28 fewer blocks than Nigel. That means Nigel has more blocks than Sally. You need to add!

	Tens	Ones
	2	6
+	2	8
	4	0
	1	4
	5	4

Nigel has 54 blocks.

Convince Me! How are these statements alike and different? Cal has 12 fewer blocks than Mia. Mia has 12 more blocks than Cal.

Guided Practice Solve the problem any way you choose. Use drawings and equations to help.

1. Lakota has 11 fewer magnets than Jeffrey. Lakota has 25 magnets. How many magnets does Jeffrey have?

?	
25	11

25 + 11 = ____

____ magnets

Name ______________________________

Tools Assessment

Independent Practice

Solve each problem any way you choose. Use drawings and equations to help. Show your work.

2. There are 28 more students than adults at the school fair. There are 96 students at the school fair. How many adults are at the school fair?

_____ adults

3. Ellie the elephant has some peanuts. She eats 49 peanuts. Now Ellie the elephant has 31 peanuts. How many peanuts did she have before?

_____ peanuts

4. The blue team scores 16 fewer points than the green team. The blue team scores 41 points. How many points did the green team score?

_____ points

5. **Higher Order Thinking** Sean studies 16 fewer vocabulary words than Chris. Chris studies 10 fewer vocabulary words than Tia. Tia studies 34 words. How many words does Sean study? Explain your answer.

____

____

____

Problem Solving

Solve the problem any way you choose. Use drawings and equations to help. Show your work.

6. **Reasoning** Kevin practices kicks for soccer. He kicks 13 times at recess. He kicks 14 times after school. Then he kicks 16 times before bed. How many practice kicks did Kevin take in all?

_____ kicks

7. **Higher Order Thinking** There are 48 red tacks and blue tacks in a bag. There are fewer red tacks than blue tacks. There are at least 26 blue tacks but no more than 30 blue tacks. How many of each color could be in the bag?

Complete the chart to solve the problem.

Red Tacks	Blue Tacks	Total
22	26	48
21		48
	28	48
19		48
	30	48

8. **Assessment Practice** Jim has 14 fewer baseball cards than Sara. Sara has 27 cards. How many baseball cards does Jim have?

Draw a line to show where each number and the unknown could be in the equation. Then solve.

27 ? 14

_____ − _____ = _____

_____ cards

Name ______________________________

Activity

Lesson 14-1

Add and Subtract with Measurements

I can ...
solve problems by adding or subtracting length measurements.

I can also reason about math.

Solve & Share

The ant crawled along the edge of this blue rectangle. Measure the total distance the ant crawled. Show your work and be ready to explain it.

Visual Learning | A-Z Glossary

Visual Learning Bridge

The book is 9 inches long and 6 inches wide.

What is the distance around the front cover of the book?

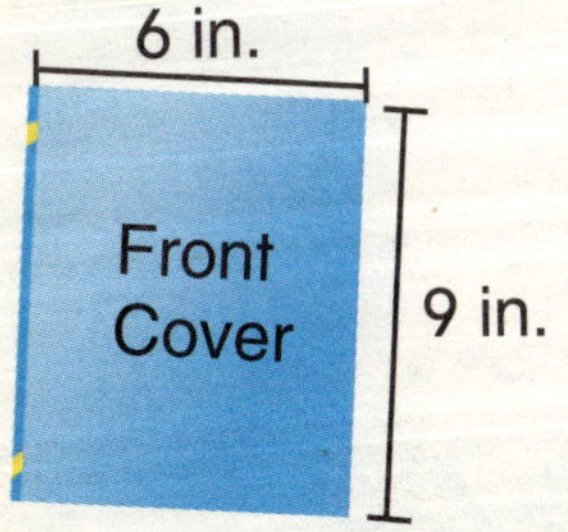

Add the lengths of all four sides to find the distance around the cover.

9 + 6 + 9 + 6 = ?

18 + 12 =

10 + 10 + 8 + 2 =

20 + 10 = 30

The distance around the cover is 30 inches.

How much longer is the teacher's arm than the child's arm?

Arm Length in Centimeters	
Teacher	66
Child	47

Subtract to compare measurements.

66 − 47 = ?

40 7 → 6 1

66 − 40 = 26

26 − 6 = 20

20 − 1 = 19

The teacher's arm is 19 centimeters longer than the child's arm.

Convince Me! Explain how to find the distance around a square park that is 2 miles long on each side.

Guided Practice

Decide if you need to add or subtract. Then write an equation to help solve each problem.

1. What is the distance around the baseball card?

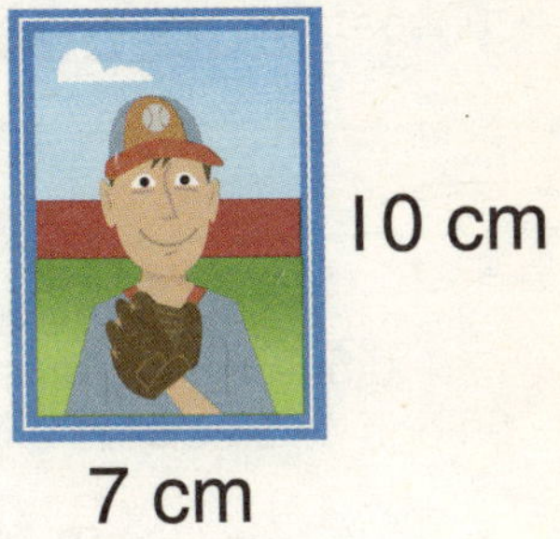

10 + 7 + 10 + 7 = 34

Distance around: 34 cm

2. What is the distance around the puzzle?

____

Distance around: _____ in.

Name ______________________________

Independent Practice

Decide if you need to add or subtract.
Then write an equation to help solve each problem.

3. What is the distance around the door?

____

Distance around: ______ ft

4. What is the distance around the cell phone?

____

Distance around: ______ in.

5. How much longer is the red scarf than the blue scarf?

____

______ in. longer

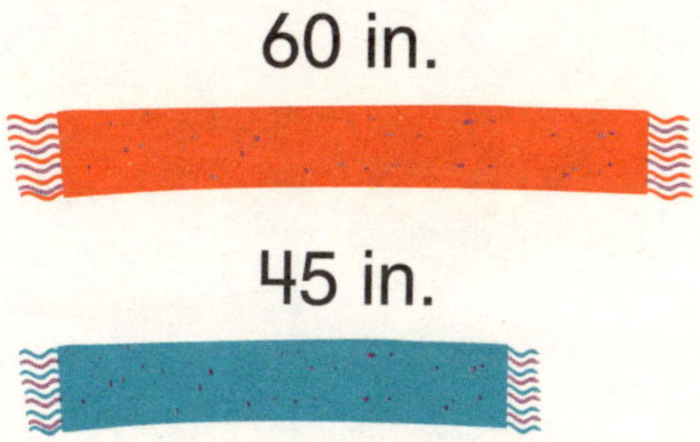

6. **Algebra** What is the length of the shorter side of the rectangle? Complete the equation to solve.

20 + ______ + 20 + ______ = 60

The shorter side is ______ centimeters.

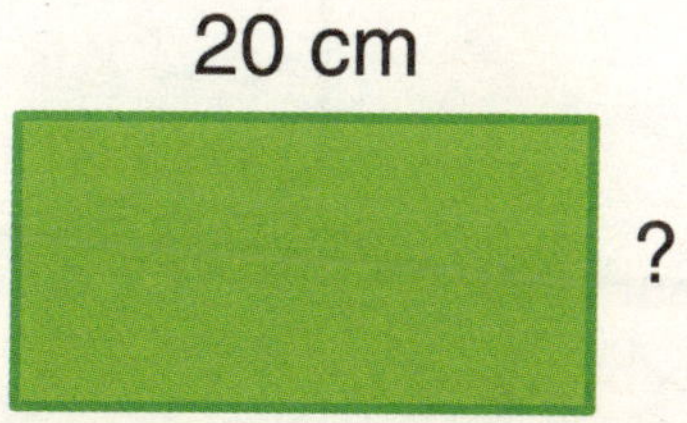

Problem Solving

Decide if you need to add or subtract. Then write an equation to help solve each problem.

7. **Model** Ashley's sunflower is 70 inches tall. Kwame's sunflower is 60 inches tall. How much taller is Ashley's sunflower than Kwame's sunflower?

_______________ _____ inches taller

8. **Model** Ben compares the length of a leaf and a plant. The leaf is 15 centimeters. The plant is 37 centimeters. How much shorter is the leaf than the plant?

_______________ _____ centimeters shorter

9. **Higher Order Thinking** Tyler threw a ball 42 feet and then 44 feet. Sanjay threw a ball 38 feet and then 49 feet. Who threw the longer distance in all? Show your work.

10. **Assessment Practice** What is the distance around the placemat?

Ⓐ 28 in.
Ⓑ 39 in.
Ⓒ 56 in.
Ⓓ 66 in.

Name ___________________________

Activity

Lesson 14-2

Find Unknown Measurements

I can ...
add or subtract to solve problems about measurements.

I can also make sense of problems.

Solve & Share

Julie and Steve each cut a piece of yarn. The total length of both pieces is 12 cm.

Measure each piece of yarn.

Circle Julie and Steve's pieces. Then explain your thinking.

____

____

____

Visual Learning A-Z Glossary

Visual Learning Bridge

Michelle jumped 24 inches. Tim jumped 7 fewer inches than Michelle. How far did Tim jump?

You can write a subtraction equation to show the problem.

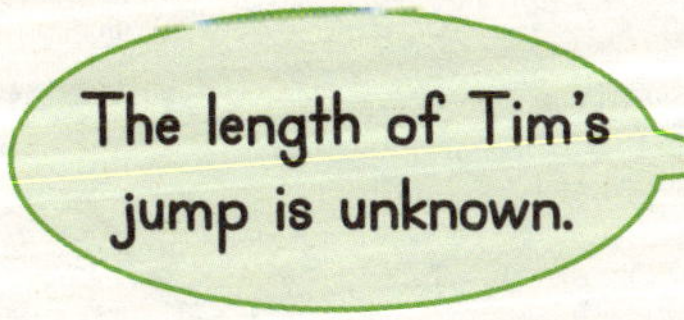

24 − 7 = ?

length of Michelle's jump; fewer inches; length of Tim's jump

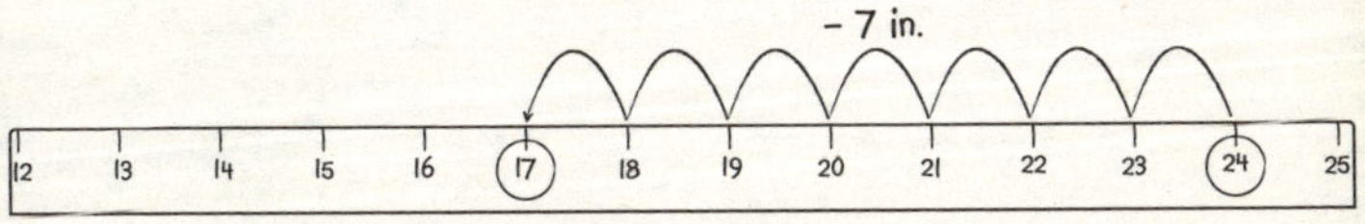

Tim jumped 17 inches.

Convince Me! How does drawing a yardstick help you solve the problem above?

☆ **Guided Practice** ☆ Write an equation using a ? for the unknown number. Solve with a picture or another way.

1. A square stamp measures 2 centimeters in length. How many centimeters long are two stamps?

2 + 2 = ?

_____ cm

2. Stuart's desk is 64 centimeters long. His dresser is 7 centimeters longer than his desk. How long is Stuart's dresser?

____

_____ cm

Name ________________________________

Tools Assessment

Independent Practice

Write an equation using a ? for the unknown number. Solve with a picture or another way.

3. Filipe's pencil box is 24 centimeters long. Joe's pencil box is 3 centimeters shorter than Filipe's. How long is Joe's pencil box?

______________________ ______ cm

4. Clark threw a red ball and a blue ball. He threw the red ball 17 feet. He threw the blue ball 7 feet farther. How far did Clark throw the blue ball?

______________________ ______ ft

5. **enVision® STEM** Ashlie's map shows where animals, land, and water are at a zoo.

The distance around her map is 38 inches. What is the length of the missing side?

8 in.

11 in.

? in.

8 in.

____

______ inches

Problem Solving Solve each problem.

6. **Make Sense** A brown puppy is 43 centimeters tall. A spotted puppy is 7 centimeters shorter than the brown puppy. A white puppy is 14 centimeters taller than the brown puppy. How tall is the spotted puppy? Think about what you need to find.

_____ cm

7. **Vocabulary** Complete the sentences using the terms below.

foot **yard** **inch**

A paper clip is about 1 _______ long.

My math book is about 1 _______ long.

A baseball bat is about 1 _______ long.

8. **Higher Order Thinking** Jack jumped 15 inches. Tyler jumped 1 inch less than Jack and 2 inches more than Randy. Who jumped the farthest? How far did each person jump?

9. **Assessment Practice** Kim was 48 inches tall in January. She grew 9 inches during the year. How tall is Kim at the end of the year? Write an equation with an unknown and then draw a picture to solve.

____

_____ in.

Name ______________________

Activity

Lesson 14-3

Continue to Find Unknown Measurements

I can ...
add and subtract to solve measurement problems by using drawings and equations.

I can also make sense of problems.

Solve & Share

Alex has a piece of ribbon that is 45 feet long. He cuts the ribbon. Now he has 39 feet of ribbon. How many feet of ribbon did Alex cut off?

Draw a picture and write an equation to solve. Show your work.

Visual Learning · A-Z Glossary

Visual Learning Bridge

A string is 28 cm. Alex cuts off a piece. Now the string is 16 cm. How long is the piece of string Alex cut off?

You can write an addition or subtraction equation.

28 − ? = 16
(length at first) (length cut) (length now)

16 + ? = 28
(length now) (length cut) (length at first)

You can draw a picture for 28 − ? = 16 or 16 + ? = 28.

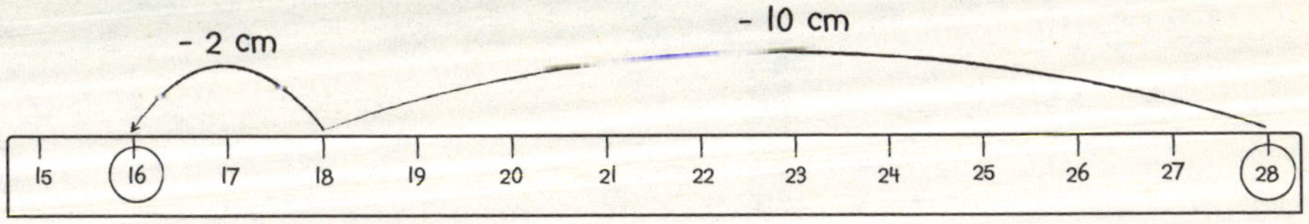

28 − 12 = 16

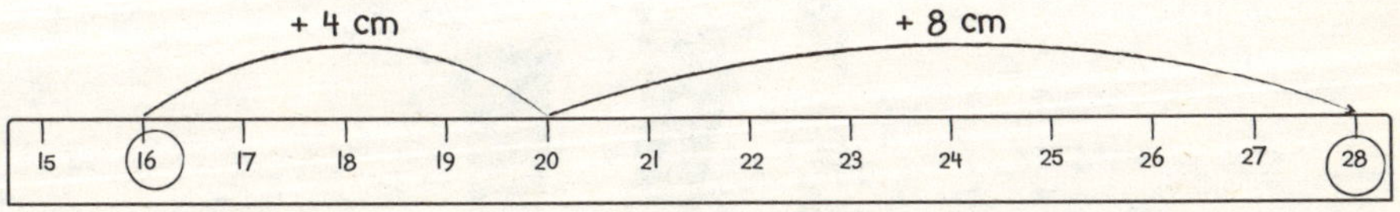

16 + 12 = 28

Alex cut off 12 cm of string.

Convince Me! How does writing an equation help you solve the problem above?

☆ Guided Practice ☆

Write an equation using a ? for the unknown number. Solve with a picture or another way.

1. A plant was 15 inches tall. It grew and is now 22 inches tall. How many inches did the plant grow?

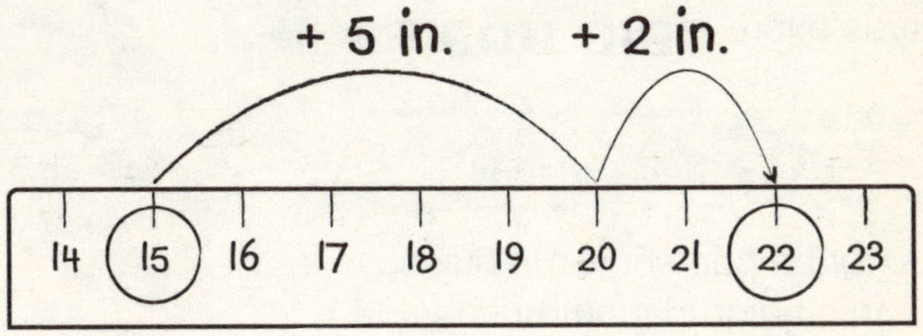

15 + ? = 22 ________

2. Each bus is 10 meters long. Each boat is 7 meters long. What is the total length of two buses and two boats?

________ ________

Name ______________________________

Independent Practice

Write an equation using a ? for the unknown number.
Solve with a picture or another way.

3. Brent's rope is 49 inches long. He cuts off some of the rope and now it is 37 inches long. How much rope did Brent cut off?

______________________ ______________

4. Sue ran for some meters and stopped. Then she ran another 22 meters for a total of 61 meters in all. How many meters did she run at first?

______________________ ______________

5. **Algebra** Solve each equation. Use the chart.

○	=	12
☆	=	39
△	=	42
□	=	57

○ + ☆ = ______

□ − ☆ = ______

☆ + △ + ○ = ______

Problem Solving

Solve each problem.

6. **Make Sense** The yellow boat is 15 feet shorter than the green boat. The green boat is 53 feet long. How long is the yellow boat? Think about what you are trying to find.

Write an equation to solve. Show your work.

_____ ft

7. **Vocabulary** Steve measured the length of his desk. It measured 2 units.

Circle the unit Steve used.

meter **foot** **centimeter** **inch**

Lori measured the length of her cat. It measured 45 units.

Circle the unit Lori used.

centimeter **yard** **inch** **foot**

8. **Higher Order Thinking** Lucy's ribbon is 1 foot long. Kathleen's ribbon is 15 inches long. Whose ribbon is longer and by how many inches? Explain your thinking.

____

____

____

____

9. **Assessment Practice** Mary's water bottle is 25 cm long. Joey's water bottle is 22 cm long. Ella's water bottle is 17 cm long.

Which statements are correct? Choose all that apply.

- ☐ Mary's bottle is 8 cm longer than Ella's.
- ☐ Joey's bottle is 6 cm longer than Ella's.
- ☐ Joey's bottle is 3 cm shorter than Mary's.
- ☐ Ella's bottle is 8 cm longer than Mary's.

Name ______________________________

Activity

Lesson 14-4

Add and Subtract on a Number Line

I can ...
add and subtract on a number line.

I can also model with math.

Solve & Share

Amelia walks 18 blocks on Monday and 5 blocks on Tuesday. How many blocks does she walk in all?

Use the number line to show how many blocks Amelia walks. Then write an equation to show your work.

Visual Learning · A-Z Glossary

Visual Learning Bridge

Amelia walks 17 blocks before dinner. She walks 8 blocks after dinner. How many blocks does she walk in all?

You can use a number line to add lengths.
First, show the 17 blocks Amelia walks before dinner.
Then, add the 8 blocks she walks after dinner.

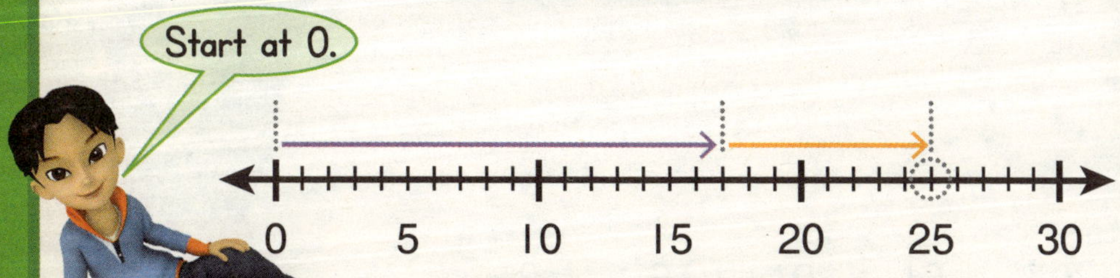

17 + 8 = 25 blocks in all

Amelia buys 17 feet of rope. She cuts off 8 feet of rope to make a jump rope. How many feet of rope does she have left?

You can also use a number line to subtract lengths.
First, show the 17 feet of rope.
Then, subtract the 8 feet of rope she cuts off.

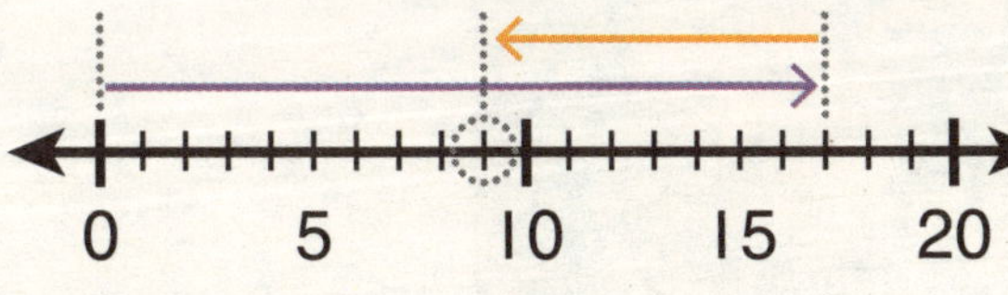

17 − 8 = 9 feet of rope left

Convince Me! Explain how to add 14 inches and 11 inches using a number line.

Guided Practice Use the number lines to add or subtract.

1. 21 + 7 = 28

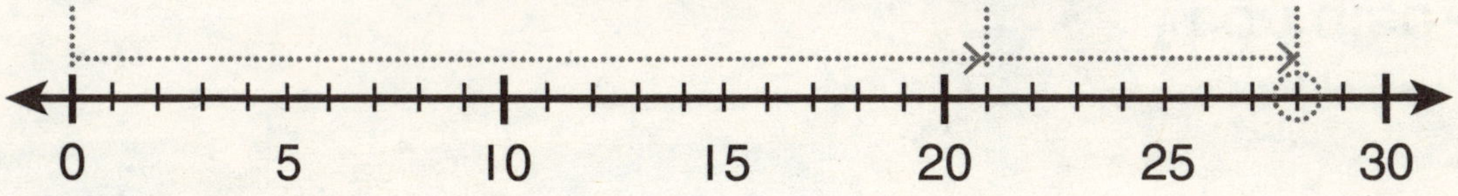

2. 28 − 14 = ____

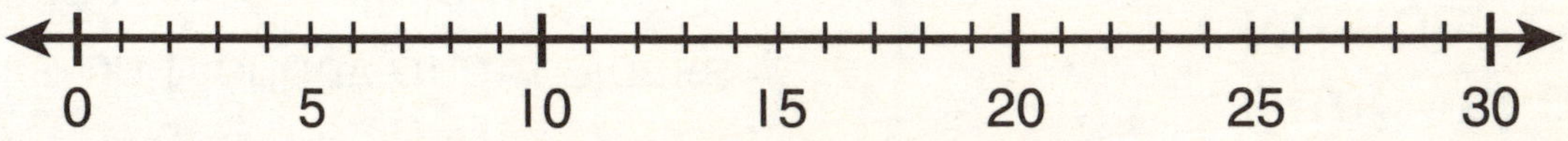

Name ______

Independent Practice

Use the number lines to add or subtract.

3. 80 − 35 = ______

4. 19 + 63 = ______

5. **Higher Order Thinking** Use the number line to show 15 inches plus 0 inches. Explain your thinking.

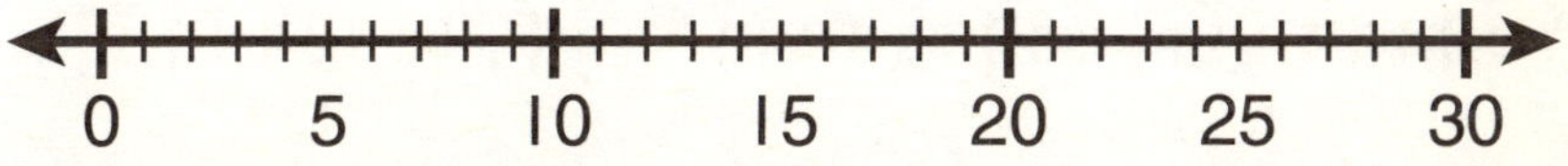

______

6. **Number Sense** Show each number below as a length from 0 on the number line. Draw four separate arrows.

9 14 24 28

Problem Solving

Use the number line to solve each problem.

7. **Use Tools** A football team gains 15 yards on its first play. The team gains 12 yards on its second play. How many yards does the team gain in two plays?

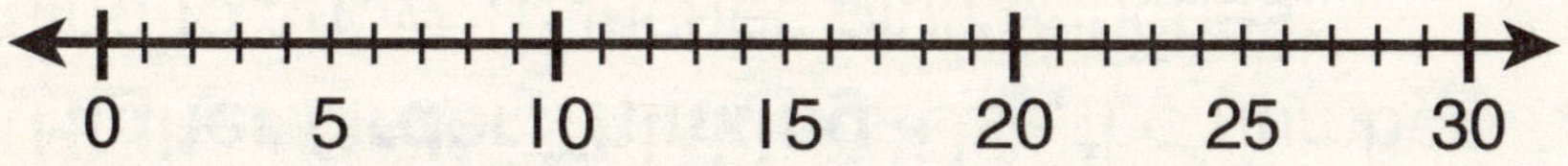

______ yards

8. **Use Tools** Mia buys 25 feet of board. She uses 16 feet of board for a sandbox. How many feet of board does she have left?

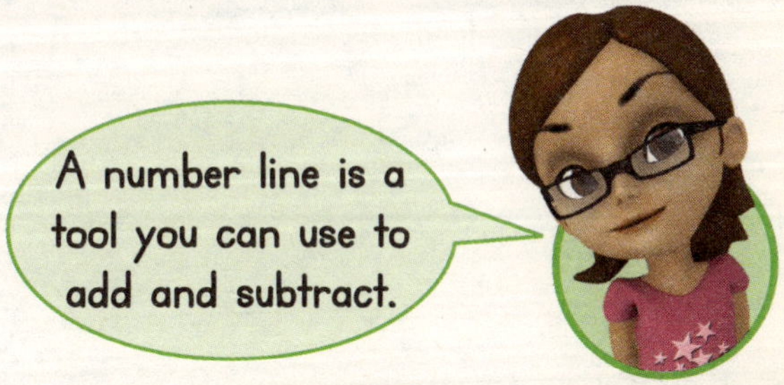

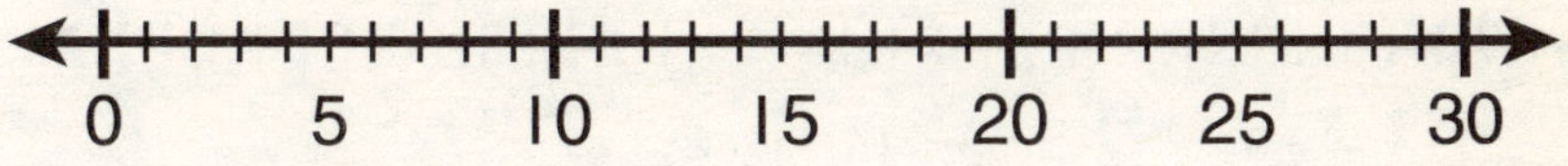

______ feet

9. **Higher Order Thinking** The runners on the track team ran 12 miles on Monday. On Tuesday, they ran 6 more miles than they ran on Monday. How many miles did they run in all on both days?

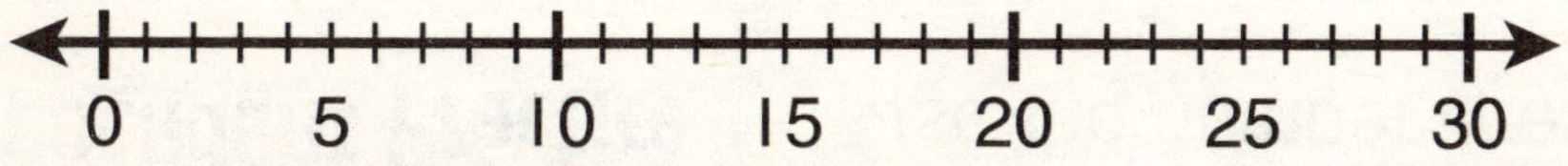

______ miles

10. **Assessment Practice** Deb has two pencils. One pencil is 9 cm long and the other pencil is 13 cm long. What is the total length of both pencils?

Use the number line to show your work.

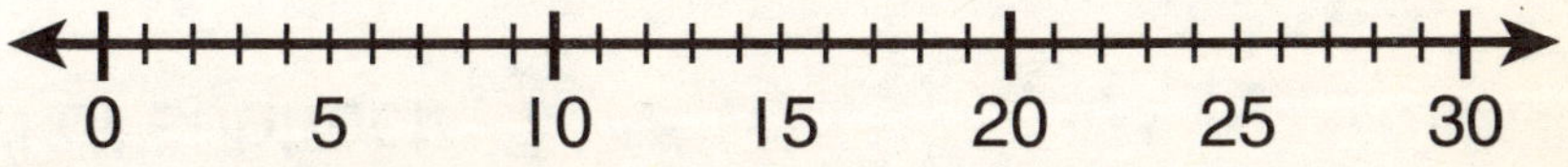

______ centimeters